PE

$\mathcal{S}tarting$ $\mathcal{A}gain$

Gillian Bouras was born in Melbourne in 1945. She worked as a teacher in Australia before moving to Greece with her husband and children in 1980. Her first book about this experience was *A Foreign Wife*, published in 1986, and this was followed by *A Fair Exchange* in 1991. *Aphrodite and the Others*, published in 1994, won a New South Wales State Literary Award in the same year, and in 1995 was shortlisted for the UK Fawcett Book Prize. *A Stranger Here* was published in 1996.

ALSO BY GILLIAN BOURAS

A Foreign Wife
A Fair Exchange
Aphrodite and the Others
A Stranger Here

GILLIAN BOURAS

Starting Again

PENGUIN BOOKS

Extracts from Theodore Zeldin's *An Intimate History of Humanity*,
published by Minerva/Reed, London, 1996, appear on pages 144–45.

Penguin Books Australia Ltd
487 Maroondah Highway, PO Box 257
Ringwood, Victoria 3134, Australia
Penguin Books Ltd
Harmondsworth, Middlesex, England
Penguin Putnam Inc.
375 Hudson Street, New York, New York 10014, USA
Penguin Books Canada Limited
10 Alcorn Avenue, Toronto, Ontario, Canada M4V 3B2
Penguin Books (NZ) Ltd
Cnr Rosedale and Airborne Roads, Albany, Auckland, New Zealand
Penguin Books (South Africa) (Pty) Ltd
5 Watkins Street, Denver Ext. 4, 2094, South Africa
Penguin Books India (P) Ltd
11, Community Centre, Panchsheel Park, New Delhi 110 017, India

First published by Penguin Books Australia Ltd 1999
1 3 5 7 9 10 8 6 4 2

Design by Ellie Exarchos, Penguin Design Studio
Front cover photographs by The Photo Library
Back cover background photograph by Stock Photos
Typeset in 13pt/18.5pt Perpetua by Post Pre-press Group, Brisbane, Queensland
Made and printed in Australia by Australian Print Group, Maryborough, Victoria

National Library of Australia
Cataloguing-in-Publication data:

Bouras, Gillian, 1945– .
Starting again.

ISBN 0 14 028148 7.

1. Bouras, Gillian, 1945– – Diaries. 2. Australians –
Diaries. 3. Women immigrants – United Kingdom – Diaries.
4. Identity (Psychology). 5. Australians – Cultural
assimilation – Greece. 6. Greece – Social life and customs.
I. Title.

305.48824

www.penguin.com.au

For Dad and Stephen

For my sons

Γιά τα φώτα μου, με αγάπη,
πάντα αγάπη

If life had a second edition,
how I would correct the proofs.
— John Clare

Ἔχει περιπέτειες, η παλιά ζωή.

It has adventures, this old life.
— Greek villager

Being meditations on age and geography,
not necessarily in that order

December

I migrated to Greece at thirty-five, halfway through the biblical span. Older villagers could not cope with my very foreign name: Julie was the best they could manage. But the name always sounds unfinished to me. When younger I went through a stage of wanting to be like the Julia in Robert Herrick's poem 'Upon Julia's Clothes', although I've not often had the chance to wear silk, so that nobody would ever be able, even if they felt inclined, to write about the liquefaction of my jeans and tartan skirts. (What a sumptuous word 'liquefaction' is.) And of course I'm much more than middle-aged now, although an optimistic English friend tells me that people these days are middle-aged until they're sixty. But Jung, who was never stuck for an opinion, sepulchrally commented that the descent begins at midday. Quite so: I've been in a free fall for longer than I care to remember.

I'm not much good with maps. Wherever I am I seem to spend a lot of time on street corners, turning the map around while trying to ensure that I am facing the right way. In spite of all my efforts, I get lost easily, but people say that Hillary and Fuchs, those conquerors of height, ice and snow, those knights of exploration, once got lost on the way to the Royal Geographical Society, an easy enough place to find, God knows, in London's South Kensington. Sometimes I forget which hemisphere I'm in, mistaking squirrels for possums, that sort of thing, and can never tell simply by looking at the sun or observing the direction of the bath water as it gurgles down the plughole. I was never any good at memorising the average annual rainfall of China or the GNP of Peru, either. Surveying mankind was a different matter: bound feet and human sacrifice were definitely more my thing.

In this business of keeping notebooks, diaries and journals, an obsession which developed with migration,

I am not alone. When the Duchess of Maslin was murdered, Charles Buller asked, 'What could a poor fellow do with a wife that kept a journal but murder her?'

Jane Carlyle kept a diary: she liked it and it was cheap.

Fanny Burney wrote her diary until she was eighty-seven, at which point 'an incapable unwillingness' seized her pen.

Anaïs Nin wanted to freeze the life that is flowing away from us every minute.

Matthew Flinders wrote his life in the form of a journal.

Virginia Woolf said that Parson Woodforde laid a magnifying glass upon the fields of Norfolk, so that every blade of grass was visible there. She also said that psychoanalysts should investigate the business of diary-keeping; she considered it the one mystery in otherwise open and honest lives.

Lady Bracknell always took her journal with her whenever she travelled, as one simply must have something sensational to read on the train.

Mae West said that if you keep a diary, some day it will keep you.

In the past my notebooks have evolved into other sorts of writing, most often autobiography. Why readers have the peculiar notion that autobiography represents the plain unvarnished truth is beyond me, but most do. The ideas of selection and omission, embroidery and embellishment seem very foreign. And foreign cultures respond in their own ways. British readers say primly, 'I could never bare my soul the way you do.' Americans complain, 'Gee, honey, I feel so frustrated. You haven't told me half enough.' To these announcements I have developed a stock answer: 'This is the autobiography I have written; you should read the one I *could* have written.' Antipodeans usually compliment me on my courage: 'Gosh, you're brave.'

'No, I'm not,' I reply, 'just desperate. Everything I write is an attempt to make myself feel better. Writing is cheaper than psychotherapy.' I do not add that I do not know whether it is as efficacious.

But it must be confessed that diarists and keepers of journals have been labelled bores, scribblers, pettifoggers and introspective annotators. At best, it has been said, they are second-rate individuals, modest, orderly and complacent, who pen speculations of dubious quality. Such thoughts always have the capacity to haunt me, and never more so than when I am in the middle of an identity crisis, an event which occurs with monotonous regularity.

The latest *crise* struck in London as I crawled away from what was called a Literary Evening, for want of a better name. Actually, I stalked off rather than crawled away, trying like mad, as usual, to present myself as the Powerful Older Woman, but my soul was crawling. Almost in the gutter. Jealousy was the problem, or one of them. The green-eyed monster favours rage in matters of the heart (I'll chop her into little bits, then him, or should I reverse the order?) and gloom in matters of the ego (nobody loves me, and this is clearly because I am not good/clever/scintillating/decorative enough to be approved of, let alone loved). But a third eye focuses on categories, and I do not belong to any. Who am I? Where do I fit? I cry, and receive no answers. Or at least I try to ignore the ones that come: Nobody. Nowhere.

The performers at the Literary Evening knew exactly where they belonged. It was clear that there are certain favoured pigeon-holes into which writers can flutter:

1. Establishment
2. Indigenous
3. Ethnic
4. Gay
5. Young

Not only did I fall into a fit of pique, but I felt insecure as well, because I cannot flutter into any of the above. One writer present could claim a very cosy place in three, for Heaven's sake. There was a lot of reading about sex, but not, it has to be said, on the subject of shopping. (Let us be fair.) Four-letter words make me flinch. (Well, there's one label for me that's not conducive to bestsellerdom: fuddy-duddy.) And then I get bored by the repetition and sameishness of them, having been conditioned to think that such repetition is Evidence of a Shallow Mind and Impoverished Word Power, and I fall to wondering whether Roget's Thesaurus would be of any help in this area of vocabulary. Right this minute, glancing over my shoulder to ensure that I'm safe from the prying eyes of my children, I have inserted a very common four-letter word into the text and then checked the relevant tool on the computer. 'Not found', comes the demure and safe answer. Well, it's nice to have some sort of company.

But I digress. Identity. Clearly there's no point in going on about the transplanted expatriate Anglo-Celt Australian category, as it's all so old hat, and in this topsy-turvy world nothing is as it was, people's disadvantages having become advantages and vice versa. In this post-modern age, identity has much to do with gaps, spaces and being challenged. I can claim many a gap and space, and there is no difficulty about meeting the challenged requirement. Visually, aurally, vertically and financially challenged, that's me. Also joint-challenged, now that my way of life is fallen into the sere and yellow leaf, and linguistically challenged, particularly in Greece and Britain. In Australia kind people like my brother suggest intensive speech therapy, for, they say, I do not sound Australian any more. (Well, I never did speak the way my uncle did, never sat having a cuppa, a ciggie and a bikkie while doing the crossie.)

In my early days in England, I once irritated an academic intensely by using the phrase 'chip bag'.

'Madam,' he intoned, 'kindly leave your Antipodean

appellations, misnomers, convolutions, inaccurate des-
ignations, call them what you will, *behind*, Down
Under, in the Wide Brown Land, in *Terra Australis
Incognita*.' He always sounds rather like a crossword
clue; I do not hold this against him, but deliberately
become Ocker and use Strine in order to annoy.

'No worries, mate,' I smiled. 'Grouse. A *crisp
packet*, right? Goddit, have I?'

'You have indeed, as you so quaintly put it, goddit,'
and he bared his teeth and rolled his eyes.

I pointed out that *incognita* was stretching things a
bit these days.

The only thing I can say is that at least I'm not fol-
lically challenged, although some of my hair seems to
be transferring itself to my upper lip. A moustache is
exactly what you need if you're going to be a good
Greek granny, I'm told: friends are such a comfort.
No, my greyness is rather a chromatic threat, I suppose, although I tell myself that Old English sheepdogs
don't feel threatened; they run up to me with glad
barks of recognition.

Certainly my Greek sisters-in-law, dyed to a
woman and every last follicle, heartily disapprove of

my badgerlike locks and tell me so one lunchtime.

'Why don't you do something about them?' they hiss. (The word for *hair* is plural in Greek.) 'Look at our handsome brother: you have to admit the contrast is a bit much.' And I do look at him, the Greek Dorian Gray, who, irritatingly, is hardly grey at all. He turns other people grey instead. I glance away again, feeling not grey but yellow, as in jaundiced, and wonder why I do not tell these Peloponnesian females to mind their own business and attend to their figures. There is, after all, a lot to attend to, as both are at least a stone over-weight. I'm scared of them, that's why; they have me bluffed, as I've never been a match for the yelling and screaming that has always followed any show of spirit. I shed tears in the loo instead, feeling completely demoralised over lunch. I'm almost always demora-lised over breakfast, but that's different.

Age: I'm tired of hearing how the young need encouragement. Of course they do, but they have youth on their side, when all is said and done, and the rest of us haven't. We get forgotten when we're having a second crack at life in an endeavour to do some of the things we wish we'd done earlier, when we're trying to reinvent ourselves. We need more encouragement than anybody, say I. Instead we wind up in a creative limbo, unappreciated, without labels, categories, *sans* everything, especially superannuation: we've been thrown out of the Literary Evening of life. Matthew Arnold said that what you have to say depends on your age, but few people seem to think that anyone over the age of forty has anything worthwhile to say, so there we are, abandoned and bombinating in the void. And feeling sorry for ourselves.

Geography: I've migrated twice, despite my lack of skill with maps, and now find that a gypsy lifestyle is forced upon me. Once my heart was merely divided, but now geographical strain has helped to break it, as have various people, and a broken heart is the heaviest kind of luggage. I became a wanderer years ago, for many reasons, most of which were connected with a basic culture clash which I despaired of: it showed little sign of evolving into any sort of harmony, and left me with a crippling sense of emotional, psychical and spiritual isolation. A dreadful polarisation had taken place, or perhaps had always been there: pioneer/ peasant; nonconformist/Orthodox; the supremacy of the individual/the supremacy of the group; introvert/extrovert; nomad/settler.

Then there was the inescapable fact that each culture has its own truth. Jesting Pilate was wise not to stay for an answer to the question, What is Truth? because there isn't one. But the long list headed *Culture Clash* could easily be added to.

Another major item on the agenda was my late development. Females growing up in the Australia of the '50s and '60s, particularly those raised in the tradition of nonconformity, were every bit as sheltered and controlled as the average Greek village girl, and were carefully trained to ignore the promptings of the heart unless these were the sanctioned ones: marriage, home, children. Duty was the thing. So was patriarchy. I can see now that though I rejected my own received life, I had still been conditioned by it, so that I unwittingly but unerringly chose to become trapped in another pattern, which was from the first devastatingly unfamiliar, and remained so. How controlled we are in our youth, while believing ourselves to be free.

Greece's proudest boast is its invention of democracy, but to this day there is little of this tradition in the agricultural, patriarchal south. Engaged in a long-delayed adolescent rebellion as I am, and living my life in reverse, I now feel myself to have been not much more than an incubator and housemaid in a situation of little equality, one with no room for flexibility or growth. But had I felt loved and appreciated rather than misunderstood and excluded, things might have been different, although I concede now as I could not concede in the past that we cannot always be loved as we want or need to be. After a long, long time, the worm finally turned and wriggled away, for fear of being crushed entirely, but I have since learned painfully that the worm that turns and seeks its own piece of earth is never forgiven. 'Begin as you mean to go on' was a rule I never learned, or had to revise too late.

Geography was also important. Always. It seems to me now that white Australians have been forced by geography to look to the future: their very act of voyaging was the sturdiest possible declaration of faith in what was to come. But for many a European, in particular returning migrants, the vision of the future is a vision of the past and its certainties. They yearn for both and for the place as well, and so they come back to the spot on the map, the *patritha*. The rest of the world is shut out, and the threat of uncertainty with it.

My mother, a wise woman, remarked more than once that the pull of a family, home and religion becomes stronger as one ages. The consolation of formal religion is something I do not have, is for whatever reason denied me; my family is now irrevocably changed by death, loss and substitution, and I am no longer sure where home is. I have been unsure of this for twenty years. Home used to be a person, and is no longer. Even when I was raising my children in the Peloponnesian village, I was always operating on the edge of things, with communication breakdowns occurring more often than I care to recall, leaving me with the defeated sense that I was never going to advance to understanding in the Greek culture. I kept on fighting my corner with failing strength and spirit, but eventually became very resentful at being surrounded by demanding men of varying ages, who in their turn became quite resentful when the resident housemaid showed the occasional sign of intelligence or assertiveness. Nobody understood. I, however, understood that a Greek village is a bad and dangerous place in which to be depressed.

In the end, the pull of a familiar culture became too strong. But I could not go back to Australia for reasons connected with geography, that old tyranny of distance, and economics. And in the long, long time that I had been away, Australia and Australian society had changed. For better or for worse, I do not know, and veer between these two opinions in my usual wobbly, indecisive style: much depends on what I hear, observe or read at a given moment. What I do know is that I have not been part of the changes. And that makes all the difference. I also consider that we are all racists in our hearts: what is familiar is almost always better, particularly as we age.

So eventually I came to London, which is a place I could recognise, at least up to a point, even if I do not seem a part of it either. But it represented escape, and more than escape: it represented what I wanted and what I had been denied, a place, no matter how tenuous, in some sort of spiritual home, and I hoped it was going to satisfy the demands and needs of my imagination. And now it is a supreme irony that I have acted in exactly the same way as any returning migrant: Britain is just as much my ancestral past as mountain villages are to the Peloponnesian peasant. Another irony is that the Greek graft took: I keep on going back to the village where I have spent more than half my adult life. I stubbornly persist in this pattern, even though I fear the gulfs may finally wash me down and that there are no Happy Isles to be found.

If our lives are stories I have three different plots, three discontinued narratives, and an impossible time-scale to come to terms with, plus a leitmotif of strain and anxiety that I do not now seem able to live without. I am a triangle, but cannot decide whether I am equilateral, isosceles or scalene. Post-modern anthropologists, however, would consider me regularly other-defined, defined by what I am not. I am not Greek; I am not English.

New Year's Eve, and I am in a bone-shaker of a bus rattling along the road to Kalamata (as in olive, south-west Peloponnese) with the express purpose of buying my favourite brand of Greek diary. With such a diary one has the comfort of knowing, for example, that Saints Konstantine and Helen share their Feast Day on May the 21st, the Dormition of the Virgin falls on August the 15th, and that warrior St Dimitrios is honoured on October the 26th. On every day of the year it is possible to remember one or more saints. The Orthodox, secure in the endless flow of history, aware that the saints are protecting them, are never alone. I am not Orthodox.

Anything can happen during a bus trip. Once, a driver sent his conductor to light a candle at a wayside chapel. More recently I had a free ride because it was the driver's name-day: mindful of his *filotimo*, he was obeying the iron rules of hospitality. Today an old man places a billycan full of milk right at my feet. It is clearly up to me to prevent it from spilling, as he can't bend over to save his life. There is a constant buzz of chatter: the talk is of relatives, of marriage, birth and death, politics and earthquakes. Everybody knows everybody else. I am the only foreigner, still a tourist and a stranger after three decades spent in a Greek world, after nearly two spent in the Peloponnese itself, and in a village at that.

The wind is whipping the olive trees. I gaze out the

bus window and observe miniature statues on the gateposts in the next village: elephants with trunks upturned, boys entwined with dolphins, the chocolate-brown concrete kangaroo decorating the house of a returned migrant. The conductor passes along the aisle, asking in trusting fashion whether everybody has bought a ticket. I become geographical and comparative and reflect that even in this occupation styles vary from country to country. One summer's day in London, an Afro-Caribbean conductor gave voice to her impatience with the hordes of tourists crammed into her Bayswater Road vehicle. 'Questions! Questions!' she exclaimed, good humour only slightly tinged with exasperation, tight curls bristling. 'Doesn't anybody understand that I have to go home and write *lyrics* after this?'

Then there was the laconic driver of a Melbourne bus who flicked his long blond locks to one side and said, 'Gotcha ticket?'

'Here it is,' I said, feeling middle-aged and anxious, having been away too long.

'Triffic,' he replied, as he clashed first gear.

I am known in the book shop; people beam toler-antly as I kick my shoes off and climb on a chair in order to check the titles on the top shelf. I climb down clutching, as well as my diary, a volume called *The Hundred Best Greek Poems*. Modern Greek, that is. And later find in it a Kavafis poem I have not read before, and over which I sniff and sob. '*Why* do you read things that make you cry?' G, the father of my children, asked once, in genuine bewilderment. I tried vainly to explain that I don't necessarily know when or if I am going to cry, it just happens. Men, worse luck for them, haven't a clue about women's lachrymal glands and the stimuli to which they are sensitive. Oh well. *Keria*. With bitter accuracy the poet sees life as a row of candles, with the future ones lit and the past ones snuffed out, malformed and twisted. The last verse: 'I do not want to turn to see them, and I am horrified at/how quickly the dark line lengthens,/how quickly the snuffed candles multiply.'

The diary I have just bought is for appointments and lists of books read; the real diary/journal/notebook is scrawled in cheap jotters with severely strained spiral backs. They sprout, these volumes – different bits of paper stuck on, clipped in, stapled.

The question of sanity apart, why do I keep a journal, particularly when I suspect that all the things I write are unsuccessful attempts to say something else? Do I write letters (and I write a lot of letters) for others, and the journal for myself? It's not as simple as that, for often letters are very much for the self, are vessels into which a great amount is poured, the recipient being merely an object which fills a gap in the correspondent's imagination, rather than a person of actual flesh and blood. A correspondence can be a meeting of minds when bodies are too timid to meet: people tell me that life is the thing, but I prefer writing.

Sometimes, though, letters are a safe and skilled way of propelling people into life. Once, a certain William Duncan of Aberdeen proposed to Alice Campbell of Argyll by letter. It was a very Scottish letter, full of good sense, very precise, orderly and methodical, and it pointed out all the advantages of the suggested union. At the end of it, the canny William wrote to Alice, 'But of course the sum and substance of this letter is your own dear self.' And of course Alice accepted his proposal, and they migrated to Australia; I like to think that they lived happily ever after.

Virginia Woolf confessed to being of great interest to herself. So she should have been, and thank God she was. For geniuses like Woolf, journals were a record of raw material, a kind of well to be dipped into, and were also a record of an extraordinary internal and external life. Boswell, that biographer/diarist supreme, wrote, 'It is unpleasant to observe how imperfect a picture of my life this journal presents. Yet I have certainly much more of *myself* thus preserved than most people have.' For us lesser mortals, engaged nonetheless in intangible pursuits, journals, notebooks, diaries give some sense of direction, are all attempts to sort things out; they are also security blankets. The journal as journey: both words have the same root in Latin and come to us through the Old French.

There is a voice that nags me, telling me constantly that I ought to write in my notebook every day. This is the sort of tyranny I strive to resist: a nonconformist upbringing, with its compulsions disguised as virtues, has much to answer for. And now, the human brain being the flighty creature that it is, I remember my adored Mr Macallister, who taught me during my fifth and sixth years at school. He was also superintendent of the local Presbyterian Sunday school, to which place I trotted dutifully every week for more years than I care to remember. Fate had really conspired against me: there were two barbed-wire fences of authority twisted around the growing girl. Mr Macallister never permitted anybody to write a sentence beginning with 'and', and he was at a loss whenever I failed to bring my needlework, which I loathed, to school. He looked at me more in sorrow than in anger on more than one occasion.

'One day,' he intoned, 'when you have children of your own, you will regret these wasted hours.' (It was sewing day again and I had come without my sampler for the umpteenth time that term.)

If I ever meet him in that Great Classroom in the Sky, I shall say, 'Good morning, sir. Now that we meet again, I feel I should tell you that I still love you to bits. You were a gentleman in your earthly life: you were kind, courteous and conscientious, and you had the courage of your convictions. You taught me grammar, you taught me how to write a proper sentence. Every so often you inspired me. But you did not teach me to love sewing, because nobody ever could, and I do not regret the hours I did not spend on it. And for a large stretch of my earthly life I lived in a place which wore me to a frazzle, but did have the blessing of a tailor who would mend trousers and replace zippers for next to nothing. I like the peculiar justice of it, don't you? The shape?'

And I see Mr Mac shaking his head and saying, 'But you were always quiet and obedient, well, except on sewing days. Your Young Worshipper's book nearly ran out of sticker space. Now you're up here talking your head off in an unfamiliar accent, *and* I hear a note of rebellion. This really won't do, you know.'

'Won't it?' I hear myself mutter, because I've had enough of the blackboard approach to life and death, and aim for the cloud where my grandfather is sitting. Of course he's wearing his tweed cap, but his fishing-rod is missing; perhaps he dropped it in the Styx.

'Hello, girl,' he greets me. 'At last I can fold away my telescope,' and he explains that he has been watching me for decades, not without some trepidation. 'You haven't wasted your time,' he announces, 'in spite of what some people may think. I knew you wouldn't. You've changed, though, haven't you? And things have been tough from time to time.'

'Yes, well, that's life,' I reply. 'And Dud,' I add, reverting to the pet name I invented for him while

22

learning to speak, 'I'm sorry you died before I had a baby; I'm sorry you died before I wrote a book.'

'Doesn't matter. I knew you'd get around to doing both. Been keeping a weather eye open, so to speak.'

But he who has a pen has a war, said Voltaire, in comparison with whom I am like a caveman who has accidentally stumbled across his first slate pencil, which has then very unexpectedly unleashed some sort of antediluvian holocaust. In short, my biro has often got me into trouble. Some people love being written about; others simply hate it and react violently when part of a journal wanders into a book and they find themselves, quite against their will and expectation, being propelled onto such a public stage. When this happens, I find myself in a state of puzzled but clearly naïve dismay. How could a security blanket have become so dangerous?

My fourth book threatens because it is fiction, but certain people are sure to deem it faction instead. It will be published in October; November will probably be the month when my battered corpse is found, weighted with stones and lumps of concrete, in the Greek river Nedon. Or in the Pamisos, which has a swifter current. I have already incurred the wrath of a connection by marriage because of another piece of writing. I fear that Zoe would like to make mince-meat of me and see the reduced result, wrapped in cling-film, reposing on a polystyrene tray forever. I have taken to wearing several Eye of God bracelets in order to reduce the power of her basilisk gaze.

When Jo, my youngest, was five, he said I should get a proper job, one which entailed wearing an orange overall and working as a checkout lady at a certain supermarket. Today, when I have a terror-induced moan about Zoe and her temper, he says, 'Well, I tried to warn you, didn't I? All those years ago. If you'd listened to me then, you wouldn't be in all this bother now.' I subside. I know I won't have the courage to take Zoe on. I would like to be able to think of myself as Superwoman, roaring and raging, fighting for truth, justice, life, the Australian way, money and *me*, but I am much more like mild-mannered Clark Kent, and tend to stay in the phone box. Nor do I take my glasses off.

For women the writing of a journal, an activity

which can be fitted into chinks of time, is evidence, surely, that they have done something other than cook X number of dinners and engage in the routine drudgery which romantic souls like to term making a home. Of course raising children is the noblest work anyone can do, when it goes right, but it is also the hardest. The little pests will insist on doing their own thing, are constantly wilful, and who can blame them?

Diarists may be bores; they are also megalomaniacs. Control freaks. And addicts, as all writers are. NB Trollope: 'Pray know that when a man begins writing he never gives over. The evil with which he is beset is as inveterate as drinking – as exciting as gambling.' Keepers of journals don't even have to obey the rules, as long as they can write a reasonable sentence.

We write to be loved, we write from motives of revenge, we write to repair our damaged selves, we write to cure our sicknesses in our books, we write about life in order to go on living it. Writing is a weapon against loss. It is also a method of pain control. Any writer attempts to fill the gaps, to adjust the balance, to shape the world more favourably. Blow reality, he says, and take this: my version is better and easier to live with. Writing is a defence mechanism. Like humour. Like irony. Like perfect manners. Like garrulousness, the relentless chatter that staves off the threat of intimacy. A journal, in particular, provides some sort of link between inner and outer worlds, both of which can be very frightening landscapes. Charting them, in a kind of geography of the emotions, no matter how unsatisfactorily and inexpertly, helps to reduce the terror, and enables us to go forward, because a journal provides us with at least some dim idea of where we have been. There is also the process of self-discovery to be considered. Thomas Fuller described it better than most when he said, 'Who hath sailed about the world of his own heart, sounded each creek, surveyed each corner, but that there still remains therein much *terra incognita* to himself?'

Keepers of journals are limpets: they cling on. They are squirrels, too, hiding things away and bringing them up to the light in wintertime.

I must have a kind face: I am asked the time and street directions in three countries, am appealed to by beggars wherever I go. I am asked to *help*. Even when I was an impoverished and very young student, an old man used to lie in wait for me on my way to lectures and ask me for a spare bob. 'For methylated spirits,' said my father disgustedly. 'He's got a tin of boot polish at home, mark my words.'

Today, at the Kalamata bus stop, a concerned daughter asks me to look after her mother, a tiny wizened creature who is racked with anxiety at the thought of a forty-kilometre bus journey. Will I please tell the bus conductor where her mother wants to go? Well, of course. While waiting, I am interested to observe that my charge can read; this fact makes her something of a rarity in her age group. She peers at each bus and recites the name of the relevant destination firmly and with a pleased air of accomplishment. She is also not a widow, being dressed in a skimpy blue dress which is vaguely matched by a patterned headscarf, tied under her ears and at the back of her head rather than under her chin. Experts can tell a woman's origin by the way she ties her headscarf; bourgeois women, the young and upwardly mobile do not wear them at all.

I stand aside to let her enter the bus, but this will not

do. She shoves me up onto the step and makes it clear that I have to haul her up and in. This is accomplished, she is stowed in her seat, her destination mentioned, her fare paid. Now the inquisition begins. It turns out that she has a connection in the village, which is nearly always the case. But she can't place me. She knows a bit about Australia, though. (Nearly everybody does and it's nearly always the wrong bit.) A good life people have there, she announces. They don't have to work, at least not very much. She doesn't hear the hollow laughs I hear echoing from a great distance.

She asks about my children, about their father, about my parents and siblings, about my work and about the annual average income of the family. She also wants to know the size of my dowry. Fool that I am, I still feel on the defensive and sheepish when this question is asked. 'I didn't have one,' I say, but add hastily, 'but I've worked for wages nearly all my married life.'

'Oh well, that's all right then,' she concedes, 'but tell me now, do these villagers love you, seeing that you're foreign and all?'

'Well, I don't know,' I flounder, and try to explain

that I keep a low profile, that I don't bother people. 'I don't say much,' I add.

'That's because you don't speak Greek,' she says. I fall silent. What have we been speaking for the last half-hour? I ask myself. Of course what she means is that I don't speak Greek the way she does, a fact that is self-evident.

She asks me my age and says how young I look. (I feel about a hundred.) She is seventy-five and looks ninety. Eventually I prepare to alight and she makes all the ritual wishes. But finally, the formulae cast aside, she gives me a dazzling smile and says, 'We are joined now. We have mingled.' I am aware, yet again, of the unsatisfactory nature of translation.

A little later a spectacular double rainbow hangs over the village, joining it from end to end. It lasts for twenty minutes, a farewell to the old year.

January

At dusk on New Year's Eve I begin my inexorable decline in a depressive spiral, beset by thoughts of past and future. The present doesn't appeal too much, either. Why did I have to find and read that Kavafis poem? Tonight, though, there is no choice but to trot off to a neighbouring house where the New Year is ushered in amid the usual atmosphere of card-playing, noise, confusion, ritual kisses, screaming babies, warm champagne in tumblers, and constant repetitions of *Chronia Polla*, Many Happy Returns, to which I respond weakly. But I have always appreciated the ritual cutting of the *vasilopita*, the New Year's cake, at midnight, with the reservation of slices for Christ, his Mother and the head of the household, who is, of course, always the husband and father.

On New Year's Day there is still more eating, as life in rural Greece in these fast-closing years of the twentieth century consists largely of Ordeal by Food. I get quietly drunk on retsina amid the screaming babies and in the process recall that one of my sons once started a school composition with the line 'I spent New Year's Day filled with bitterness and inconsolable grief.' I try not to dwell on this recollection and instead make three resolutions, two of which are plainly silly and piecrust promises to myself. I resolve:

1. To give up drinking ouzo.

2. To give up worrying about my wrinkles, on the grounds that some people love bloodhounds. British bulldogs don't have a bad following, either.

3. Never to put my pride in my pocket again.

This last, of course, is the big one. Write off the bad investments, I say to myself bracingly. Too little return. People must now make efforts for you.

In the morning I am sober.

My big boys are on leave. Tom is doing the dread military service and Mick is on his way to becoming a commando sergeant in the Greek SAS. They are glad to see me and the washing-machine. I remind myself how much I love them as I ponder a new definition of Hell. Hell is twenty-three khaki socks; at least Tom has the grace to present me with his offending items carefully tied up in a plastic bag. The missing sock remains missing.

Tom is now a corporal and assisting a colonel in the declassification of documents, which means he will have to sign a form promising not to leave the Hellenic Republic for six months after his discharge. The Greek army is just as inspired as any other, it would seem, when it comes to putting the wrong person in the wrong place. Tom is a talker, a yakker *par excellence*, one who loves life's rich pageant, the players, mummers, the whole gang, and who cannot resist commenting on anything. The idea of him working with secret material is ludicrous, almost as ludicrous as the idea of his learning to use an anti-tank missile during the six miserable months he spent on the island of Samos. The secret Turkish weapon, I thought him. He is totally unmechanical and now boasts of having the rustiest gun in the army. He's much happier in Athens: no more shaving in Coca-Cola, for one thing.

My mother-in-law, the redoubtable Aphrodite, is dying but is being very slow about it. She always did have a will of her own, our Yiayia. Now she and a prominent politician are crawling neck and neck towards their meeting with Charos and Cerberus and the trip across the Styx. But they are hard to kill, both of them, are not in the business of giving in or giving up. In the dying stakes Yiayia is doing better: she's at home, in familiar surroundings, and seems to be comfortable enough, drifting in and out of what we are pleased to call the real world. Of course, she must know somehow that her children, bound by silken cords of love and obligation and reflexes conditioned by generations of teaching that this-is-the-way-you-do-it, will care for her and her immortal soul as long as they have breath in their own bodies.

The politician, tubes leaking from every orifice, has had a tracheotomy and is comatose in an Athenian hospital. Crowds of the party faithful camp on the hospital steps. I am bemused by this, but remember that crowds also gathered at the gates of Buckingham Palace in order to read the bulletins about the condition of the dying King George V. I can't help thinking, though, that there is a world of difference between hereditary monarchs and flighty politicians, and between the measured elegance of the sentence, 'The king's life is drawing peacefully to its close,' and the medical and journalistic babble emanating all too often from Greek television.

George V was a quotable old coot. I particularly like his 'I may be uninspiring but I'm damned if I'm alien,' and have occasionally and conceitedly fantasised about reversing it for the edification of various locals.

Mick is into discipline, Tom into having a good time. Back in Athens he rings me, huffing and puffing as usual: gotta get the old adrenalin pumping, he tells me. He cannot live without drama: Irish and Greek genes mingle attractively but exhaustingly.

'No postman comes to this section of the Greek army.'

This is an excuse, but I make suitable tut-tutting noises.

'The loos are so awful that I use the ones at the railway station. Sometimes they forget to feed us.'

This is really serious stuff, but being the worst mother in Greece, I am not about to start sending food parcels. I change the subject.

'How's the colonel?'

'He's okay. Not a bad bloke, but he wants me to coach him for his English exam and I know he won't pass. The sky would be full of flying pigs if he did. He also wants me to learn to type by tomorrow.'

'The only thing I know about typing in Greek is that you put the punctuation in first.'

'Punctuation? I can't even get the paper in straight.'

'Isn't there a manual?'

A faintly disgusted sigh greets this naïve question. 'You never learn, Mum, do you? Stop being so rational, for God's sake. Of course there's no manual.'

'Just asking,' I reply huffily. 'Hope springs eternal and all that. Usually there's a knob on the right-hand side of the carrier —'

'Yeah, yeah.'

'What does the colonel say about your efforts?'

'He says things like, "You're stuck, Corporal, aren't you?" And I have to stand up and salute every time he comes and goes.'

'My heart bleeds. Think of the Hellenic Republic.'

'How can I *avoid* thinking of the Hellenic Republic, Mum? Get real.'

'Yeah, yeah,' I mimic, laughing like mad. 'I'm going to write all this down now.'

'Well, that's just lovely. Go and make a few bucks out of your eldest son's suffering. Go on.'

'I've done it before,' I riposte brazenly, and ring off.

The gypsy woman who pushes a handcart through the village passes by and I purchase knickers at a bargain rate. I am grateful that she doesn't press me to buy other garments, as I am a soft touch, although toughening up with age. My nonconformist soul saved me once, though, I recall, when I refused to buy a bead that had supposedly belonged to St Ekaterina. That gypsy's price began at fifty thousand drachmae and dwindled to five, but I stood firm while Mick, then aged eight, was white-faced with terror.

'Buy it, Mum,' he urged, 'or else she'll steal the baby.'

'Do you think so?' I asked eagerly. 'No, no such luck. She's bound to have six of her own.' Mick looked wounded and hurt and the baby chortled in ignorant bliss.

Jo is now back at school after the Christmas holidays, which means that I can do wicked things like read detective novels in the morning. On his return at mid-day I ask stupidly, 'What did you learn today?'

'Nothing,' he replies succinctly.

The winter of my discontent. Well, which winter wasn't? At least the sun shines quite regularly, but the price to be paid for this is recurring heavy frost. The house is very cold. All day long I trek miserably between the wood heap and the kitchen, keeping the stove fed and my fingers cracked.

The wood heap is a microcosm: rats, snakes, worms, woodlice, centipedes, millipedes, spiders, they're all there in season. And the archaeologists will be entertained: on one occasion, when the heap was getting low, I discovered an antique pair of boxer shorts and an equally antique bath plug. The wood heap is also a goodish place for reflection; I stand momentarily to extract a splinter or six and wonder who in the village would possibly believe in my several visits to the House of Lords, all of which have happened by chance and have been interesting, to say the least.

With a stern effort I try to forget the champagne on the terrace, the cream teas, the sonorous tones of debate. I remind my socialist soul that the institution is totally undemocratic and the place itself reminiscent of an elderly citizens' club, almost the equivalent of the village *kafeneion*. While waiting nervously to be met on the occasion of my first visit, I heard an ominous creaking. Earthquake! my displaced inner voice shrieked in terror, but no, it was only an elderly peer moving slowly through the foyer. Later, in the chamber, I observed two members sleeping soundly. My companion informed me afterwards that another was picking his nose, but in all honesty I have to record that I did not see this. Still, one can probably get away with anything if one is a lord.

All inbreeding, eye-patches and receding chins, I tell myself even while yearning for the comfort, dignity and decorum so signally lacking on the wood heap. At which point Ozzie the dog leaps out in a frenzy of his kennel – in reality a draughty and collapsing crate – dashes to the top of a crazy pile of olive branches (definitely not the peace-making sort) and roars a challenge to the neighbour's dog, a nastily aggressive collie who regularly becomes bored with life as shepherd's assistant.

I help the spider immigration programme by carrying a pile of wood into the kitchen. The Peloponnese seems to be the preferred abode of trillions of daddy-long-legs and other species besides. The former wander amiably around the bath, while the others spin webs so assiduously that de-cobwebbing could take place every twenty-four hours, and should. But it goes without saying that the whole house often resembles Miss Havisham's bridal chamber, de-cobwebbing taking place only when the spirit moves me, which is not often.

The wattles are blooming in mad profusion, and I fight a futile rearguard action against the English foreign wives who will persist in using the word mimosa. Everybody is harvesting olives and the hills are alive with the sound of chainsaws, but the almond trees are already misted in white, the purple ranunculi are springing up everywhere, and so are the mauve-edged white crocuses. Wisps of cloud layer the mountains, the sunsets are pink and dramatic, and Greece is so beautiful and this lonely crowded life so unfair that I could scream. I cry instead, late at night, in an unedifying welter of self-pity and homesickness for various people and places, in bed.

There is no change in Yiayia's condition. The waiting season is upon us.

Today is Australia Day. Expatriates do all sorts of peculiar things they would never do at home, and so I attach the miniature flag given to me by my parents so long ago to my very utilitarian broom handle and prop the lot, secured by a few strategically placed bricks, in a corner of the top balcony. (An Australian I know of in Staffordshire flies his flag upside-down because that is the way Australians would see it if they could; people drive up to his door to tell him what he already knows.) It is a dull windless day and the flag droops sadly, but I feel constrained to take a photo nevertheless, and am squinting and peering with my camera and still in my dressing-gown when Jo trots down the front steps on his way to school.

'Do you think I'm mad?' I ask.

'As a cut snake,' he replies without a moment's hesitation, and continues down the path. At least one corner of the Peloponnese will be forever Australia.

The swearing in of the new Prime Minister, a ceremony telecast direct from the presidential palace in Athens. The elegant room is full of Greek men, very few of whom can be said to match the room. The PM is neatly suited and wears a bold red tie and modest grin. There are two women present and only two. Flashbulbs pierce the mist of incense as a gold-sashed deacon points the way in the *Evangelio* while the Archbishop reads aloud. Said Archbishop looks ancient. Of course celibacy has no pleasures, but the Orthodox Church has many pains, usually of the two-legged, black-robed, stovepipe-hatted sort. No wonder the top brass look old before their time.

The PM is the best choice, according to my sons and their father, none of whom wanted the candidate it pleases me to call Kyrios Chocolopoulos. This appellation amuses them and also reassures them that the state of my Greek is still abysmal and that I am definitely racist in my preference for names of only one or two syllables, or those that are hyphenated: ones that I can pronounce without effort, at any rate.

The anniversary of my mother's death. Months ago, in an outburst of renewed grief, I pinned a collage of photographs above my desk, so that there she is, ageing from twenty-five to seventy, a beautiful brave woman, always humorous, always spirited. She smiles from the wall and I hear her say, Keep on, keep at it, and I cannot do otherwise, because she always kept on, because she never gave up. All shall be well and all manner of things shall be well, she instructs. Not for nothing were her grandparents from a village near Norwich. We'll see, won't we? I reply, grinning in watery fashion at her various images; if I try very hard I can remember her as she was at twenty-five.

The Greeks and Turks are at it again, disputing a bit of rock in the Aegean. 'It's not just a bit of rock, Mum,' says Jo. 'It's got goats on it and the people of Kos and Kalymnos use it.' Goats, sheep, rocks, flags – nothing is worth your brothers' lives, I think, but remain silent. The headmistress of the *gymnasio* Jo attends is the very one who told his brothers that every man must be prepared to shed his last drop of blood for *Ellatha*. And now here we are, with both big boys in the army. Please God, I say, striking a quick bargain, I don't mind how many khaki socks I have to wash as long as nothing comes of this. In fact I don't mind anything. God gives me the treatment I deserve: silence.

A retsina-clouded lunch and a resolution to stay away from the television set get me through one day.

On the next I go to the post office. Early, as usual: it is so important to know as soon as possible whether one has been totally abandoned or not. Postmaster Theo grins at me and says, 'Jittery, eh? Don't be. Remember that this sort of thing has happened before and will, without doubt, happen again. Flags, for the sake of *Panagia*, our all-holy One! This is the way we are, we Greeks and Turks. We don't seem able to help ourselves.'

Reading helps me. I read seven detective novels the week I returned from London. 'You're addicted, Mum,' announced Jo.

'Yep,' I agreed. Once I told G about an Australian writer I know who reads two hundred and fifty books a year. He glared. Greek men are good at glaring. 'That only goes to show that she never does any work,' he said flatly. I do plenty of what he terms work, in my incarnation as housemaid, and also move away from the detective novels. A tome called *Women and Marriage in Victorian Fiction* is truly appropriate reading in the Peloponnese. And having put off reading *The Fortunes of Richard Mahony* for thirty years, I can now boast that this particular gap has been plugged. Mahony is a nomadic, indecisive, migratory man I feel I understand, seeing that he is irremediably torn between Britain and Australia, but it's a sobering thought that he winds up quite insane before he dies. Well, that's expatriates for you.

Expats are not the full ticket, a London taxi driver told me once. I laughed. Ruefully. But I have been told that I am not an expat, I am a migrant, and there is a whole world of difference.

FEBRUARY

The month of Aquarians, wearers of amethyst as protection against violent passions. Sensible Aquarians. Pisceans, whose month this also is, have rule over the feet. Funny, that, seeing fish haven't got any. But the few Pisceans I know are capable of pretty fancy footwork, in one way: they bite shark-like chunks out of you and then swim away. I am a Leo. Really I'm no lion, but rather Kipling's cat, wandering along, biro and notebook in paw, on my wild, wild lone. A bracing sort of bloke, Kipling, with that sensible idea of treating those twin impostors good and bad luck as if they were the same, the moral lesson being, I presume, what one does despite luck. Kipling also said that there are only two sorts of people, those who stay at home and those who do not.

To the hairdresser's, late in the day. The hairdresser's place symbolises my rather ambivalent attitude to the world, I think: I don't want too much of it and its complications, I don't want to venture into it too often, but I want to know it's still there, spinning away. I gird my loins, as it were, because these visits fall into the category of Fascinating Ordeal, and have not changed their power to daunt me over the years. Nor have I learned to relax.

It is, the hairdresser's place, in its small and primitive way, the equivalent of an eighteenth-century French *salon*, for women only. Women's solidarity in Peloponnesian villages is doubtless fascinating to anthropologists, and to more ordinary observers as well. In this older generation there is rarely any sense that a woman has a need or liking for the *company* of men. Just as well, really, as it is rarely forthcoming. Village marriage is a straightforward business transaction, hallowed for all sorts of emotional and psychological reasons by the sacred example of the Holy Family. Both husband and wife want children, for life is meaningless without them; the man provides the economic framework, and the woman supports and comforts him, the master builder. Only romantic, idealistic Westerners seem to persist in aspiring to a few extras: companionship/understanding/intellectual stimulation/emotional support/fun/all of these. Greek village women have the Church to turn to and the company of other women.

In the winter they linger longer than necessary, these women at the hairdresser's, gathering round the wood stove, enjoying its heat and that given off by the antique dryer into which their hedgehog skulls, bristling with rollers, will be inserted sooner or later. In summer they sit on their doorsteps, their tongues and crochet hooks clicking in unison as the perfume of jasmine wafts through the evening air, as rose beetles wheel and dive in the deepening shadows.

Today seven women greet me politely but reservedly, as they have always done. They are not certain of my age, but somebody in my advanced state of greyness should not be wearing jeans. Strictly speaking,

I should never even wear trousers, for I am the daughter-in-law of a priest. The fact that I never met him, the fact that he has been dead more than twenty-five years, the fact that my mother-in-law now inhabits a twilight world in which she does not register me or my clothes, has no relevance to this matter at all. But then I'm foreign; what can one expect?

They are getting ready for Candlemas tomorrow, and so they sit waiting in turn, ankles crossed, hips spreading over most uncomfortable chairs, hands clasped, headscarves removed against the imminent attentions of Panayota. In her all too premature widowhood, Panayota has taken to religion with a fierce intensity. She has a glorious mane of white hair which today, newly washed, is spilling down her back, determinedly escaping the black plastic combs with which she attempts to anchor it at regular intervals. She has great drive and intelligence, great vivacity, and is one of the most graceful dancers I have ever seen. But she will never dance again; as for the rest of her virtues, where is she to make use of them? Nowhere but in the service of a male-dominated church which does not deserve or appreciate the gifts she has to offer.

We go back a long way together, Panayota and I. When I was confined to bed for nearly three months after Jo was born she would come into the house to cheer me up, admire the baby and trim my hair. We have talked about our losses. I remember her newly widowed, I remember her cry of pain: 'Where are they now, these people, the dead?' It is the only time I have heard her wonder, and I feel now as I felt then. I wish I knew; I wish I could tell her the answer.

Panayota stands and snips conscientiously and with flair. She knows what she is about; she has been cutting hair since she was twelve. The scissors clash to the accompaniment of tape-recorded music from a church in Nafplion. '*Oraia*,' she breathes, '*then einai?*' Beautiful, isn't it? The seven heads nod and then the chattering is resumed.

The moment I entered I observed with dread the presence of ageing, fearsomely plain Stella, the self-styled female intellectual of the village. This afternoon she looms over me, tickles my more than incipient dewlap with a hand which would be the envy of many an Australian brickie, fixes me with her gimlet gaze and proceeds to catechise me. This procedure shows signs of developing into a sport, for she has engaged in it before and a pattern is emerging. She quizzes me about my religion – What do Protestants believe? – makes me feel a heathen, asks me what the established church of Australia is, and then begins to tell me about Luther, at which point I gather the tatters of my self-esteem about me and inform her frostily that I *do* know something about Luther. But she always has the last word. Are you a good person? *'Kalos anthropos?'* she demands to know.

I collapse again and mutter something ineffectual about trying to be. Such self-doubts and half-measures are not Stella's style: she knows she is a *kalos anthropos,* and leaves at this point, wishing us all good health – *yeia sas.* I retire gratefully into silence and listen to the other conversations.

Panayota has moved from a discussion of the faults and shortcomings of the Orthodox clergy to a consideration of the faults and shortcomings of Greek roads. On other occasions she has informed me that I should be preparing myself for the next life.

'I'm not ready,' I say. 'There's too much to do and too many problems in this one.'

'*Ax!*' she exclaims. 'This is no way to think.' Self-doubt is not Panayota's thing, either: in fact, it seems to be in fairly short supply in rural Greece.

A fine day for Candlemas, and in Kalamata the feast day of the cathedral is being celebrated. The sunlight will make shafts of light shoot from the crowns of at least six bishops. Hundreds of priests will form a long, multi-coloured crocodile behind the most sacred icon of *I Panagia*, All-holy Blameless Lady, as it is paraded through the streets accompanied by black-clad choristers and white-clad girls strewing rose petals. Nothing ever changes.

It is not a holiday in the village and so I routinely visit the post office and am treated to the not unusual spectacle of the postmaster losing his temper. He roars and bellows, but on this occasion refrains from throwing the telephone around the room. I am the only person affected by this show of rage, at least as far as I can judge. My stomach knots and I feel sick, suffering from the 'never make a scene, dear, always be a lady' conditioning that it is too late for me to shed or conquer. Each culture has its own way of coping.

I: I must behave like a lady and be polite and calm.

He: I must behave like a man and show this lot that I am not to be put upon, not ever, and I shall make that very clear.

I relinquish my role as court jester to Tom, who has a couple of days' leave and regales me with tall tales and true of army life, of how the minute the commanding officer leaves they do what they like, and how one of their number was nearly caught smoking pot when the officer returned early and very unexpectedly, and how the officer brings his mistress onto the premises: then the door of the inner sanctum is locked for hours at a time. I wonder again why the Turkish army does not attempt a regular monthly attack, but then it is not clear to me what shape it is in.

Some of Tom's stories have the capacity to boggle the mind of his dinosaur mother. Boredom was reigning in the usual fashion one morning, he said, when a beautiful young woman walked in. 'An absolute stunner!' breathed my son reminiscently. 'There was a bloke with her, but we didn't take much notice of him, that's for sure. The sergeant, just an ageing villager, poor old thing, nearly fell over himself to be polite and obliging. There we were, all panting, when she asked to see the army doctor. We thought that was a bit funny.'

'Oh yes,' I said, slow on the uptake.

'Hell, Mum,' he boomed. 'She, he, it, was a trevally!'

'I think I get your drift,' I ventured, 'but I thought a trevally was a fish.'

He sighed. 'You've missed the bus, Mum. Way behind, as usual. Trevally is slang for transvestite. But actually, I suppose the person had moved onto the next stage. What is the next stage? What's the word I want?'

'Transsexual?' I hazarded, hoping to prove that I was not such an ignorant old bag after all.

'Yep, you're right. How do they manage it, anyway?'

I told him the little I know.

'Hmm. Strange. Heck, Mum, in this case, what a criminal waste, what a crying shame.'

'Oh, I'm sure you all felt that.'

'The sergeant was the worst. He was flabbergasted.'

'What happened in the end?' I asked.

'Well, it seemed she was quite happy to serve the Hellenic Republic.'

I laughed; my son clearly did not understand the ambiguity of a certain verb. Thank God.

'And?'

'The Hellenic Republic said thanks but no thanks. We do draw the line somewhere, Mum!'

Conversations with my youngest, who has a neat way with an aphorism. His latest: good manners are not always convenient or helpful. Now it appears that he doubts the existence of both God and the Devil, and thus beset by doubt waxes briefly philosophical. 'Nature does what it does, man does what he does, and the universe does what it does.' He pauses briefly. 'But,' he says, 'who invented the universe?'

'A big question,' I remark.

It so happens that later in the day we watch a programme about supernovas, which are apparently very observable from the middle of Australia. 'Here we go. Heresy,' I comment cheerfully.

'Interesting, though. Oh, I don't believe in Heaven, either.'

'What, no harps, wings, sitting on clouds and all that?'

'Nah, boring, boring, boring.'

'Have you told Papayeorgi all this?'

'Yeah, right.' (As heavily sarcastic as only a fifteen-year-old can be.)

'Are you still going to confession and taking communion?'

'Yes.'

'Why?'

'Because I have to.'

So much for my strand in his inheritance, with its emphasis on individual conscience, the 'here I stand, I can do no other' lesson that was drummed into siblings and self in that dusty little weatherboard church, with its wooden lace and blue fleur-de-lis carpet, ten thousand miles away. I still rather incline to the view that there must be a strip of that same carpet leading up to the Pearly Gates. But then at his age I had not questioned anything, my parents had only just acquired a black-and-white television set, and far from knowing about supernovas, I feared the end of the world was imminent simply because my grandmother, who knew the book of Revelation inside out, said that the olive groves were once more flourishing in what had been Palestine, and that the time (as well as every possible olive) was ripe. My grandmother made me a teenage insomniac and lost not a wink of sleep herself. She knew she was going to her Saviour: she was all right.

Children still fear the end of the world, I suppose, but in rather a different way. The end of the world is now seen as being much more man's responsibility than God's. Some time ago, Jo decided he was going to write a short story in the horror genre. It was about Horace the pig. The setting for this nascent epic was Peru, and somewhere in the wilds of South America Horace was to have the misfortune to fall into a pool of toxic waste, after which he would become some sort of mutant and begin eating people at a great rate. It was interesting for me to recall and compare: the first writing of any length I did as a child was a novel set in Scotland. As I had not been any further north than the Wimmera district of Victoria at the time, my knowledge of Scotland was roughly on a par with Jo's knowledge of Peru. I can recollect no plot, which would seem to suggest that there wasn't any; I have a vague memory of romance, and I know that the whole thing swashed a good buckle, and that there was certainly no mention of toxics and mutants. It had a very short life and petered out after ten laborious pages.

Horace remains a mere figment of Jo's imagination.

One of my Greek ex-students has just paid me a visit. We talked of many things, including weighty matters like Life and Change. She feels she no longer knows her Athenian friends, for she has been out of Greece, lived other days, known other ways, and they have not.

'They criticise me because my sink is not shiny,' she said sorrowfully.

I chuckled sympathetically, having failed many a sink test myself.

'I really believe', she announced, 'that it is the little things that count, that make the difference, because the big things happen to everyone.'

She is right when it comes to the corrosive nature of a thousand disappointments, but big things such as Love and Loss can make an enormous difference, can change an individual world irrevocably. She is very young still; she will learn this lesson, I hope not too painfully.

For Peloponnesian villagers the idea of fun is foreign and suspect and timetabled for Feast Days only, and I have often wondered whether my attachment to this part of the world has something to do with the dour nature of the Presbyterianism from which I am sprung. The idea of payment having to be made, and punishment, was never far away, and still is not: God punishes this part of the world with the occasional earthquake. For village people, for the most part, Life is Grim, Life is Earnest, and a matter of What Will People Think? How the myth of the light-hearted Mediterranean ever got off the ground is a complete mystery to me, even though a witty friend suggests that it was invented by the first Englishmen to spend their holidays on the French Riviera.

Poet and mystic William Blake had his own view: 'It is the Classics, and not the Goths nor Monks, that desolate Europe with wars.' He didn't mention the sex war; perhaps he forgot, or wasn't interested.

I am leaving for Athens and for London tomorrow. It is a difficult period, and I am on the rack of the 'don't want to go, don't want to stay' emotions that seem to have been part of me forever. There are the inescapable facts of my half-Greek children and this place, this damned place in which I have spent a very long time. I am quite unable to say goodbye and equally unable to solve the mystery of Greece's attraction. It's a complex sort of mystery, I know that: the landscape, the weight of history, the vitality of the inhabitants and the fact, for me, of time. I've twined some of my roots around rock, have had to become like ivy. And now, when a length of ivy is ripped away, tiny pieces of rock cling to it, and will not fall off.

It is over twenty years since I first came to Greece. It was not love at first sight; rather, it was bewilderment at first gasp, and the bewilderment has never quite gone away. I still reach out to clutch at essential truths about the place, and am left, very often, with only a surface impression, which may have changed or disappeared by tomorrow.

Long, long ago I wrote that Greece is like that other jewel of the East, Shakespeare's Cleopatra: age cannot wither her, nor custom stale her infinite variety. It is true, yet part of this truth is that Greece is forever unattainable, so that she is also like the Spoonmaker's Diamond in the Topkapi Palace Museum, winking and revolving, blinding and beckoning, but always at a distance, with a sheet of glass a permanent barrier. And different facets catch the light continually.

I once heard of a woman who blamed Gerald Durrell and his *My Family and Other Animals* for her addiction to Greece. But Durrell, like most writers, simply did what he had to do. People like this woman succumb to the temptation to reinvent themselves. People like me – who am I fooling? But it turns out, eventually, that the passive voice triumphs: in the end we are reinvented by forces beyond our control. At this stage of my life I could find it in my heart to blame Robert Louis Stevenson and his idea that the great thing in life is to be on the move.

I hope tomorrow will be wet and dreary, but I fear, really fear, that it will be sunny and bright. Today I do what I usually do as part of my routine when going away: I go on a long walk to the very end of the village, or to one end of it, where the chapel of St Nikolaos marks the outer boundary. A little white structure, it sits and broods over a view of olive groves, cypresses rising like sentinels, and terracotta-tiled roofs. It was in this church that G's father, the priest, denounced the communists during the Civil War; his bishop removed him with all speed to a safe seminary in Corinth.

The blood-red poppies are beginning to appear. Once I thought they only ever bloomed in Flanders fields. But Greece has eleven different varieties of red poppy. The purple ranunculi and crocuses and wild irises are now multiplying madly. 'Never mind,' said Lesley, an English friend, a few days ago. 'The bulbs will soon be starting in London.' And so they will, but at this moment I do not care very much. I am trying not to think of Henry James, who once remarked that London was 'a mighty ogress who devours human flesh'.

Nothing alters in this routine. I talk to black-faced

sheep and scratch their noses through wire fences. The bent old women shuffle along the lanes and eye me sourly. Here everybody has to fit, and I do not. *Yeia sas*, I say, doing the right thing. Sometimes they reply, sometimes they don't.

The next day is not bright and sunny, but reasonably mild and cloudy-grey instead. The bus rolls on and up through the Peloponnese. In Arcadia the gorse is in bloom already. Thick fog wraps the bus between Megalopolis and Tripolis, and we inch along until we enter the tunnel that now cuts off the Argos section of the journey, with all its hair-raising bends, and emerge once more into whiteness. This soon lifts, the rest of the journey passes in a blur, and then we are all contending with the ordeal of the Athens bus station. It has hardly changed in two decades, being full of dirt, noise, carbon monoxide and rude employees. After much struggle and delay I fall into a taxi which has a sticker on the dashboard: 'I'm a taxi driver. God, please grant me restraint and patience.' Once I thought God was fluent in Greek and had a willing ear, but the antics of today's driver, which include the mandatory rip-off, convince me that God has given up Greek lessons, is illiterate, and has hearing loss as well.

Athens is a miserable place in the rain. I stand for forty minutes outside Kifissia station, waiting for an Australian girl who is suffering from unrequited love for a Greek man. Leah left a secretarial job in Sydney in order to travel. She arrived in Greece and proceeded to fall in love with everything Greek, especially Kimon, who eventually decided that he didn't love her back, or at least not enough. In the way of travelling and transplanted Australians, we have mutual friends, and so she has been to stay in the village. In her attempts to shrug off her received life and to reinvent herself, and in her susceptibility to the exotic, she reminds me very much of my young self. Leah knows no half-measures: she has to give all her heart, and that same heart chose a man who represents most of what her psyche needs. Or what she thinks it needs. And like me, she perseveres in keeping friendships green, which is why we are meeting today.

I wait and wait, feeling cold, unhappy and eventually sick with panic, for I have never been able to understand how people who have little or no Greek actually manage in this unpredictable and occasionally chaotic country. But Leah turns up. She's got herself a posh job as nanny to a ship-owning family in Piraeus. This I think very appropriate. Over a year ago I worried about the idea of her spending a fortnight's holiday under our roof. I feared there would be a veritable ocean of mixed emotion swirling about her, was afraid she would be swamped by tidal waves of male tension and competitiveness. But no: like a cheeky little yacht she survived every buffeting and bobbed up determinedly on every crest. I admired her and envied her the toughness I will never have.

I do not, however, envy her her present stage of life, which is all too distressingly familiar. I know what it is to find something precious only to have it disappear. It's a bit like fairy gold, perhaps, in being not quite real, although I was convinced of the truth, validity and reality of my particular hoard – who's to know? That conviction is probably part of the enchantment, an ingredient in the spell. Whatever the case, there is no doubt that distance is a guarantee of difficulty. There is also no doubt about the pain, humiliation and sheer helplessness involved in unrequited love.

'I wish these feelings would go away,' Leah says.

'I know exactly what they're like,' I reply, although the young think that such an assertion is absolutely ridiculous. In their view, age and love are mutually exclusive categories. Time will teach them otherwise.

'Do you think they'll *ever* go away?'

'I don't know,' I say slowly. 'There are no guarantees that they will disappear completely. Perhaps there will always be a sore spot.' I do not want to say any more.

'What am I going to do about my broken heart?'

'Ah,' I answer, trying to take a lighter tone, because I do not want to tell her that I have swept up the pieces of my own heart and put them away: they will not be needed any more. 'The only thing to do is to get yourself some bandaids and a few strips of velcro and do what you can to patch it up. Even then you may find there is some bleeding between the bandages. That's the way of it, I think. But you can rely on good old *chronos* to do at least some healing for you.'

She sighs. And while she does so, I think of my favourite quotation, a comment on love, from *The Towers of Trebizond*: 'When we were together, peace flowed about us like music, and fun sprang up between us like a shining fountain.' I once quoted this to a much more worldly friend, who said, 'You're just an old softie.'

Activity is the thing, as is the noble art of distraction, so off we set down Vasilissis Sofias in a gentle drizzle. I point out every part of museum-land; we talk easily and are both amused when a spot she claimed she knew, St Agnes, turns out to be Syntagma, Constitution Square. 'St Agnes is what the British nannies call it,' she announces defensively.

'Well, now you're one up on them, poor old Poms,' is my reply.

I say goodbye to her and then goodbye to Athens and fly through the night to London. Night flights are the ones I favour: they cost less and you don't feel you are wasting the daytime. Three months ago, flying in the opposite direction, I sat next to a man from northern

England. He was that rare species of man who does most of the work in a marriage; he was the one who was vigilant of the children, who carried one in and sat next to both of them while his wife sat elsewhere and did nothing except enjoy being waited on. He was quite good-looking; she, equally, was not. She was also very fat and only partially peroxided, black roots of her straggly hair showing. Why men like him are, even occasionally, at the beck and call of women like her, is beyond me: it's all part of the eternal mystery, I suppose. He had his mother and four sisters on board as well, which I thought explained rather a lot.

As the night wore on he was made bold by his can of lager, I by my gin and tonic. He told me they were all en route to Athens in order to attend the wedding of the youngest sister to a Greek.

'I'm not too sure why this wedding is taking place,' he meditated, gazing at his fast-emptying can. 'They've lived together for years, these two, in a nice village in Yorkshire. Stone cottage, roses round the door, all that stuff. Now she's cooped up in a high-rise flat in Glyfada, right under the flight track.'

'Stop right there,' I commanded. 'Would there, by

any remote chance and long stretch of the imagination, be a widowed Greek mother in this particular story?'

He stared. 'How did you know that?'

I sobered up instantly and decided against another drink lest it make me tearful. Then I told him a potted version of my own story, after which the questions followed thick and fast. I probably answered these all too frankly, for I remember advising him not to tell his mother of our conversation, as it might start her worrying about the daughter poised on the brink.

I had trouble placing his accent, he mine. Where was I from? Australia, I said.

'But you haven't got the accent,' he announced. Why they think there is only one I have no idea, but off I went into my worn explanation of being away for years and at present spending long periods in England.

'Oh, that accounts for it,' he nodded, sagely. 'You're educated now.'

I laughed. It seemed the only thing to do. I should have had that second G&T, after all. I certainly needed a stiff one at a later date when another

Englishman, of the relentlessly jocular type, told me about his friend in Sydney who had decided, after a lot of soul-searching, heart-burning and all the rest of it, to take out Australian citizenship. He had the operation first, I was told. I waited for it. Yes, sure enough, it came: he had had half his brain removed so he could be a real Aussie.

Here I am back in Virginia Woolf's home town, or one of them, and feeling just a wee bit peculiar. Well, at least I'm not as miserable as a bandicoot. Not yet. The first time I had a room of my own in London I did not feel at all inspired, despite a rereading of the eponymous text. I missed my children/friends/dog/house/garden/mild weather. London made me feel like the little match girl and more than a little sorry for myself. Match girl/ bandicoot. My darling Royal Mail was on strike, so that I felt personally betrayed. I ate quickly and unheedingly, and still do, cooking for one being no fun whatever. And shopping for one makes that same one feel terribly reduced, somehow, and I'm not referring to the fact of the few things in the shopping basket. I have always talked to myself, but the length and frequency of these conversations increased immediately in London, and quite alarmingly. Every morning I lifted the holland blind to peep at a monotonously grey sky and to think, What now?

Back here in yet another winter I merely feel a little inert, the way I often do in Greece. But for different reasons. In Greece there is no choice about the way one lives one's life; in London there are too many, so that initially I make none. But then I start gadding about, doing too much in between bouts of hard work. (This is a policy statement: a great many people think that my life is one long holiday.) And even when I am working obsessively hard I go out once a day. But I know a writer who holed up near a Greek beach and did not speak to anyone for eight days.

'Eight days!' I gasped when she imparted this piece of information.

'Just like a fast,' was her nonchalant comment.

When all else fails, I rush to the local supermarket in order to connect in no matter how minimal a fashion, and to say G'day to the check-out girl. I can't fast.

But right now I seem to be sitting about a lot,

apparently doing nothing. I hope to God I resemble Woolf, who said she often did her best work at times like these. That is the only hope I have of resembling her in any way. She liked being on holiday and being a guest, it seems, because of the relief of not having to order dinner.

I am at Australia House – the Downer Room, to be precise. It is a difficult room to love, and many people, even Australians, consider it the ugliest enclosed space in London. I cannot make up my mind. As usual. But I do know that Australia House is the epitome of opulent empire: over-the-top, too much of everything at monstrous expense in 1913.

This same place makes me realise that a Melburnian gypsy like me meets a much wider geographical range of Australians in London than anywhere else. 'Where're you from?' is the question on everyone's lips. 'I'm from Brizzy,' says someone brightly, 'and he's from Rocky.' I make a mental readjustment as swiftly as the ageing, retsina-sodden grey matter will allow: to me the olive groves of the Peloponnese are much more familiar than these exotic foreign parts which just hap-, pen to be in the land of my birth.

Still more adjustment is needed on the occasion when I find myself watching a stunningly beautiful videotape of the outback, the production of an English filmmaker. An Englishwoman who wears desert sand in a bracelet phial on her wrist and comes and goes between the outback and London regularly, and who has spent months living with an Aboriginal community, performs a traditional dance in celebration. There is a didgeridoo accompaniment – the instrument is played by an enthusiastic young Japanese man with dreadlocks. All this takes place, to my considerable bemusement but to nobody else's, on a grey day in an attic in middle-class Muswell Hill. Muttering to myself, I compare the didgeridoo to the bagpipes: both are definitely to be played outdoors. In London, the outdoor playing of the former is usually impossible, I realise, because of the inclement weather, for how can one blow one's nose and the didgeridoo at the same time?

Spiderwebs of thought: I remember my scientifically and statistically minded brother telling me cheerfully that the plague bacillus still lurks underground. How far down? I wonder, thinking about the tube and the Northern line being very deep. And that if the traffic in London were still horse-drawn, today's inhabitants, being as numerous as they are, would be up to their necks, every one, in horse dung. I make a mental note to tell him that a dog relieved itself today *inside* the Hampstead post office, while the patiently queuing customers stared studiously into space. Such things do not happen in Greece and Australia.

Neither does the bareness. All those stripped trees still come as a surprise to one used to eucalypts and olives. But already there is a mist of cherry blossom in evidence and in another month the tyranny of the weather, the penetrating cold, will be almost over. There is a great mental divide between those raised in a cold climate and those who have benefited from sunnier skies. Chekhov was most disapproving of the south: 'Oh my God, how contemptible this life is, with its artichokes, palm trees and scent of orange blossoms.'

Today layers of fog do not want to shift: ghostly

shapes and movements make for an unreal world in which buildings and people appear suddenly and just as suddenly disappear. But though the trees may be bare and skeined in white, daffodils and jonquils are starting to trumpet bravely, the snowdrops are massing, pink camellias and white roses are rioting, and in late afternoon, which is not very late really, a pale orange ball of sun emerges and lights up the beds of winter pansies.

There is always something to look at; there is always somebody to listen to. Today it is Mrs Bourke, the Irish cleaning lady, who is always ready to take on the worries of the world, who is a predictable mixture of faith and pessimism. She spent a long time praying for the soul of the young English girl who, some time ago now, collapsed and died in the arms of her Greek bridegroom as they emerged from the church after the wedding. 'The family are taking it up,' she remarked sombrely, 'because the Greek doctors had been treating her for a *membrane*.'

Mrs Bourke has a friend, also Irish, who cleans for a well-known playwright. The rivalry between them is intense despite being vicarious.

'My house,' said Mrs Bourke on one occasion, 'is going to Buckingham Palace next week.'

The friend could not let this pass. 'The master has an invitation to St James's,' she announced immediately, 'but he says he's not going because they won't give him a space to park his bike.'

Off to the House of Lords for arvo tea. Wot larks. But oh the weather. I crunch along the streets of NW3 in my old shoes, amid whirls and swirls of snow, blown by a biting wind. I am mortally afraid that I am going to fall. But I don't, and so duly present myself at the Peers' Entrance, where the graceful gentleman in black tails and clanking medallions, seals and gongs, shows not the remotest interest in the fact that I have my presentable shoes in a black plastic bag labelled W for Waterstone's. I could be a feminine reincarnation of Guy Fawkes, for God's sake, carrying a pound of Semtex into the peeresses' loo. After all, as one of my English friends tells me, I look exactly like a terrorist, being short and dark.

The Novelist and the Archbishop are there. They

always say G'day, I'm told. I'm so jealous of the Novelist's royalties and his ability to plot that I might not say G'day back. In any case I do not get the chance. Tea lingers into the G&T interval and I inwardly debate the possibility of stowing away in the House of Lords. It might be possible, but knowing my sort of luck I would be discovered and packed off to the Tower with all speed, to be provided with board and lodging of the bread and water variety. No lord is going to take pity on me. Anyway, it will not come as a surprise to learn that your average lord is as programmed as your average Peloponnesian peasant: only one way of doing things, no sense of adventure beyond the odd dalliance or two – odd possibly meaning very odd indeed.

Ah, but their manners. I understand their manners, having decided long ago that I would rather be attacked by a rapier than a battleaxe. Of course the rapier inflicts wounds just as deadly: the difference lies in the external appearance of the victim, who bleeds internally but does not make a mess on the carpet. In my sunset years I have a decided preference for fastidiousness and style.

As it is a leap year, this is a chance for desperate women to land a husband. The various unattached men of my acquaintance have no need to buy pairs of white gloves for my sake, as I am not at all interested in jumping from the frying-pan into the fire. Nor am I looking for a meal ticket or seeking rescue. It's a worrying fact that men of uncertain age feel threatened by women of uncertain age, and are absolutely convinced that they, the females, have dire designs on their a) honour, b) bank accounts, and not necessarily in that order. Poor old things; they've got it wrong. What women of uncertain age really want is somebody compatible to talk to and go to the theatre with: the idea and ideal of company is very seductive, particularly if you've not had much of it. Literary company is even more seductive: now, when I tell a man that I'll never cry for him again, I want him to know that the allusion is to *Great Expectations* and that when Pip says the same thing to Estella he admits to himself that his announcement is 'as false a declaration as ever was made'.

MARCH

I have spasms during which I record mere trivia. *French Granny Smiths*, if you don't mind. How dare they? And as I ponder the arrogance of the French in particular and the subject of apples in general, a picture of Wheeler's orchard, last seen in 1956, springs into my mind and I see row upon row of apple trees in the sandy red soil of north-west Victoria. Because David Wheeler was in my class at school I was allowed, on this long-gone afternoon, to pick and eat Jonathan apples straight off the tree. The apple I remember was a lot bigger than my fist. As my fist even now is not very big at all, this recollection does not mean much, but the way in which childhood memory alters proportions seems to be significant. I remember my teeth in the crispness that has never been equalled: apples were crisper, summers longer, rainbows brighter way back then. Of course in all likelihood the apples were coated thickly with DDT, but this sort of thought does not do in one's declining years.

While in reminiscent/nostalgic mood I discover an exhibition of artifacts related to Constable's *The Cornfield* at the National Gallery. This painting is a favourite with a great many people: the pundits agree that it has entered the British visual consciousness, that it represents quintessential Englishness and home. But it also means home to vanished generations of Australians, and they probably would have used a capital H.

Great-uncle Lindsay was an antique dealer in Richmond, Melbourne, which meant that the best *objets* were in the shop and the second-category items, as the Greeks would say, were kept at home. His print of *The Cornfield*, one of thousands made, was on the dining-room wall: a flock of sheep being kept in close order by a dog trails along a tree-lined lane and a scarlet-waistcoated boy lies flat out and face down in order to drink from a stream. (For years, craning my neck in order to see, I thought the boy was asleep.

In my childhood this painting was not quite accessible art.) The cornfield and a village beckon in the distance; a plough stands on one side of a hedge, a farmer on the other. A donkey and foal wait near the boy.

The great British public was invited to send in artifacts connected with the painting, and relevant bits and pieces simply flooded in: fire screens, wallpaper samples, playing-cards, thimbles, cushions, plates, even a clock with the print beneath it. Some of the people who are so attached to the painting were also interviewed, so that we have an insight into the nature of their attachment. An army officer has spent many a lunchtime at the gallery trying to learn Constable's secrets and slaving away at his own copy of *The Cornfield* in the evenings at home. One woman wanted to know what was happening beyond the painting, while someone else maintained that there was no need to ask any question or make any comment about the painting. 'My God! It's all there.' It is very strange to remember now that Constable was unable to sell this particular work.

Nostalgia is often condemned as the vice of the expatriate, or else it is seen as being indulged in by those for whom the present is not at all satisfactory. But the surprising reaction to this painting, and I'm sure it was a surprise, indicates that age and change make foreigners and expatriates of us all and that a certain amount of nostalgia is an integral part of life. People have a right to view and review the past in their own way; every so often they have an opportunity to assert that right. I have to confess that it is a relief to me to learn this.

There are an awful lot of people in London and most of them seem to adore art. Well, good, but so much the better if you are over six feet tall. If you are considerably under, the viewing of pictures becomes more than a little difficult in crowds like these.

From something like the sublime to an object bordering on the ridiculous: I have been given a pop-up card of Melbourne, a skyline to send to Jo in the village in Greece. It is shamelessly kitsch and condenses the city of my birth and youth to a piece of cardboard seven inches wide, five inches high, and three inches deep. There are five rows of cut-outs and absolutely everything is included. The Yarra is a hectic unreal blue and indeed all the colours are far too garish, but I pore over the whole creation, which is clever in its way. Let the years slide away, my mother used to say, and as I look, they do. Once more I sit in the Royal Botanic Gardens, once more I see the glint on the tent of the Music Bowl; I even feel the rattle of the trams on Princes Bridge. The ageing brain is a peculiar thing: suddenly I recall that Melbourne Grammar boarders always referred to their chocolate and coconut blancmange as Yarra mud and dandruff.

There is a woman on her own in the supermarket, really on her own, I mean. Someone has left her, of that I am quite sure. She wears no ring; her face is drawn and taut, and has a certain question stamped all over it: Is this all there is? I recognise it, having asked it so many times of myself. She seems the reserved type, and the world is not geared to them. Her shopping consists of a sandwich, hermetically sealed, which means she'll swear at it later and slash at the wrapping with a knife or corkscrew, if she's impatient like me. What else? Two oranges, three bananas and a pint of milk. Emotional upheaval has gone straight to

her stomach, that seems certain. How well I understand, for her shopping is so like my own: limited,
unimaginative. She is much younger than I am. Is this
better or worse? Most people would say better. She can
start again, they would say briskly. But it seems to me
that starting again is a matter of temperament rather
than age. I suspect that the underrated safe haven of a
marriage has just collapsed and she is at the stage of
crawling out from beneath the rubble. It amazes me
how infrequently men understand or recognise this
safe haven and how easily and carelessly they jeopardise
it, together with everything they have. I suppose some
women do this, too. I just don't know any.

My Akubra hat. What a misunderstood piece of headgear. It seems to have a symbolic value I never
dreamed of. But lately I've added to the symbolism
and have decorated it with an Anzac badge, emu feathers, and a Celtic brooch. You're a scream, said an
Australian friend who has no insecurities about her
identity. It's a beautiful hat, but it's just not you,
remarked an English friend. Friends are *so* comforting,

as I've said before. On seeing my hat an academic from Australia virtually refused to speak to me, on the grounds that an Akubra-wearer is almost always a member of the gun lobby as well. (He was clearly not a logician.) I took great offence at this, as I regard all firearms with fear, detestation and loathing. An Englishman, however, thought the hat was wonderful, and wanted to know whether I had just worn it to a wedding. (I mean, as if one would.) I wondered whether he meant a Queensland wedding, where legend has it that you can tell the bride: she's the one wearing white thongs.

It excites attention in the tube, my Akubra. Teenagers laugh at it. Older people of a certain station in life nudge each other and say, 'Get the hat.' They're only jealous, I tell myself, and glower at them. Once, when I was trudging between platforms in the company of a Melburnian friend, a man complimented me on the smartness of this pastoral model. Friend, in didactic mode, said, 'Of course you know where that hat comes from?'

'No,' he confessed, trotting by my side.

'Australia,' came the answer.

'Good on ya, Blue,' came his, as he disappeared in the direction of the Piccadilly line.

In general it proves handy for purposes of conceal-ment, as people look at it and not at me. Whenever I slink into The Body Shop to buy new supplies of spackle with which to gild the rapidly ageing lily, the Bright Young Things are intrigued and then become very helpful. In a second-hand *dress agency* in Knightsbridge I hide under my hat as I prowl timidly among the recycled Armani numbers and castigate myself inwardly for having champagne taste on a beer income. It is surprisingly noisy in the dress agency, as powerful pronouncements made in cut-glass accents soar through the air and bounce off the walls. These are the voices and pontifications of women who were bred to confidence and have never had it dented, let alone shattered. Or so it seems to me. No hiding under Akubra hats for that lot.

To the Queen Elizabeth Hall to listen to Mozart and Beethoven as played by a violinist who looks very Greek and about fifteen, a cellist who looks terrified, quite understandably, and a pianist whose dark beauty and fine bones convince me of the existence of classical music groupies. Before the trek back I dash to the loo and confront the inevitable queue; the scene is considerably enlivened by an Englishman of the vague sort who wanders in all unsuspecting. I laugh like mad. Unkind of me, but I can't help it. He shoots me a look of pure horror, turns ashen, and bolts. It's quite refreshing to see a panic attack in this phlegmatic population where the men in particular have elevated phlegm to the level of high art.

In the company of a medically minded friend who is also interested in history and entertainment of an improving nature, I visit the old St Thomas's operating theatre, which incorporates the Herb Garret, home to an exhibition of old vegetable remedies, where I am quite put off my lunch by the sight of bits in bottles – strangulated hernias and such like – not to mention the theatre itself with the large tray of sawdust under the operating table and bloodstained aprons hanging on hooks. One of my ancestral names figures in the register of surgeons. For 'surgeons' read 'butchers', way back then.

To an Oxfam shop for a casual browse. My attention is taken by a very presentable blue shirt. I investigate further and discover the label: 'HM Prison'. A strange reluctance to purchase comes upon me and I long to know how it comes to be here. Of course I dare not ask.

On the way back from the Oxfam shop I pass a popular coffee spot and note that I still have great respect for people who drink or dine alone. Today a man is sipping cappuccino while perusing the paper. He looks the soul of aplomb; I wonder if I am the only one who has observed that he is wearing odd socks, very noticeably odd to one who is the daughter of a colour-blind man and the mother of another. My mother checked my father's colour schemes every morning of their married life; somebody has let this man down. Never mind, what he doesn't know won't hurt him.

Off to Sotheby's for the very first time, in the company of a friend who professes herself quite unable to tell me why the horse paintings of one James Seymour are predicted to fetch at least a hundred and fifty thousand pounds. People here seem very happy to sell off their ancestors, but their ancestors' animals seem to bring more. I am almost totally ignorant of art (the shame of it) so there is nothing I pine to have on my non-existent walls except a portrait of a woman wearing a wonderful black hat matched by a choker. Her dress is very *décolleté* and her head rests on a hand encased in a silvery glove. She has a very knowing look. Both title and painter interest me. It: *Portrait of a Lady formerly called Kitty Fisher*. (Now, there's a mystery, at least to me.) He: the Reverend Matthew William Peters RA, 1741–1814. I suspect that a man of the cloth should not have been interested in painting the likes of Kitty Fisher but of course I could be very wrong, and just scenting a story. In any case, she is expected to fetch between two and three thousand pounds, a lot less than any horse on display. Such is art, with all its various vicissitudes.

To the Royal Society of Literature, of which I am a nervous member. As this is my first visit, I ring beforehand to ask whether I need to bring proof of membership. 'You're all right,' says the person to whom I have not spoken for four months, 'because I recognise your voice.' What this means I do not know. To a lecture on biography, a subject that never fails to draw me like a magnet.

I have the great good fortune to sit next to an elderly woman, beautiful and with bags of class, who positively shines with tranquillity and grace. Both qualities have probably been very hard won. The reserve that is part of the British stereotype is non-existent: we get talking about all sorts of matters, carefully avoiding the subject of husbands, and dwelling briefly on the subject of age. Lots of compensations, she announces firmly, because you don't care so much what people think. It turns out that she has had a classical education, lucky thing. 'I'm so glad I've read Homer,' she says. She visited Greece before the war: again, how fortunate. To have seen Athens when its population was a mere one hundred thousand, instead of the *nefos*-haunted four million of today, to have been in Greece before it was changed forever by occupation, civil war and tourism: what a privilege. She got around quite easily, although she said she couldn't speak Modern Greek. But the sentence she laughingly recalls for my sake, 'Where is Byron's house?' is absolutely correct, her accent completely comprehensible.

She is aware that her time has passed. 'I'm the last

of the amateurs; our generation could be.' Then it was question time. Did I think in Greek or English? Were I to pray (the delicacy of her phrasing I thanked God for) would I pray in Greek or English? English every time, I smiled at her. The English often find it hard to believe, somehow, that Australians are quite attached to the language of Chaucer and Shakespeare and even harder to believe that we know a bit about it. She said she had a deep attachment to English. Naturally. Then she said she could never become Roman Catholic but could contemplate becoming Orthodox. I feel the same. It has been a privilege, she says, to grow old with interesting, intelligent people.

It is my privilege, I tell myself, to be growing old with a variety of people.

APRIL

An acquaintance works with young people who have what is tactfully described as a life-controlling problem. I have one, too: an inability to remain in one place for more than a couple of months at a time. Well, I do have the ability; it's encouragement from other people that is lacking.

To Paris, where I have never been before. I have always been implacably opposed to the concept of the Eurostar train service, for my usual cotton wool, bleeding-heart liberal reasons, but I am almost immediately converted, even though the platform at Waterloo is so long I feel as if I'm walking to France, and even though the idea of all that metal racing along at 300kph makes me feel ill with fear. Not to mention the weight of the water on the Chunnel itself. A more technically minded friend assures me that a leak is more likely than a dam-burst, but I do not believe this. The thought of the cleverness of it enchants me, though, as does the sight of the countryside whizzing past the window. The train slows to a sedate speed as it goes through the tunnel, but there is nothing to see except blackness. Tunnels are tunnels. I am reminded of an anecdote involving a little boy in post-war England who finished eating the first banana of his life just as the train he was travelling on entered a tunnel. As it emerged into daylight, another small boy started to peel his own banana. 'Don't eat it, whatever you do,' the first child urged. 'Those things make you go blind.'

A glimpse of soft Parisian light before the plunge into the Metro. Suddenly I am being pushed and pummelled. The brain is a strange thing, or at least mine is. In a condition of terminal confusion when it comes to place, it immediately assumes I am in Athens and so I start to push back, never dreaming that my purse and I are parting company. I manage, on discovering this, to swing into the Pollyanna mode, albeit with difficulty, and address myself sternly. Be glad:

1. You are not alone.

2. You did not lose more money.

3. You were not mugged.

4. You have been taught to be more careful.

But I have lost my favourite photograph of my mother.

I am here so briefly that all I do is accumulate a blur of images: the gleam, glamour and precise coordination of officer and horse near L'École Militaire, the regularity of the neat rows of bare trees along cobbled streets, the pale wash of sunshine, the fearsome boil of traffic, the *bateaux-mouches* on the river, the glint of gold on Les Invalides. But the little tablets on houses and corners marking the spots where Parisians fell during the war remain very clear.

On a later visit I take in more: Sainte-Chapelle, built in the thirteenth century to house the relics of Christ's Passion, most notably the Crown of Thorns, bought for a monstrous sum from the Emperor of Constantinople, with its rich gold, ruby red and royal blue and the effect the light has on all these. Then there is the effect that plainchant has on me, brought up as I was on psalms sung in metre. I know nothing about these things but have a dim feeling about the merging of chant and building, the utter appropriateness and matching of song and place.

Notre Dame and its doors and its gloom and glass and sad notices warning 'Beware of thieves' in several languages, the sobering thought of the child labour that helped to produce this solemn, weighty miracle. The exquisite symmetry of the Place des Vosgues, its rows of sculpted trees and colonnades. The bridges of Paris, the walk from the Arc de Triomphe along the Champs Élysées, the wandering in pale morning light in the Luxembourg Gardens, all the touristy things I have waited so long to do.

I visit the Australian Bookshop, where the proprietor has been less than enchanted to hear an Englishman remark in the street outside, 'I didn't know Australians read books.' It seems we are still meant to be amused by this puerile nonsense.

To a Corot exhibition. I seem to be working my way up from Constable and James Seymour. His portraits I approve of, also the landscapes, and Corot's feeling for the shapes and directions of trees, flowing and windswept, the scenes viewed through a veil of delicate foliage, but I cannot say I warm to the vast canvases like *Saint Jerome in the Desert* and *The Destruction of Gomorrah*. But these huge things, so I'm told, were the prize-winners of the day.

I am bold enough in large places: it's the small places that bother me, so that I cringe when I make a grammatical error in Greek in the village. Here I am simply amazed when my creaking, cobwebbed French is understood. It *is* amazing, when I recall that I was taught by three conscientious Australian men who travelled to France only in their yearning hearts and imaginations.

With postcards to the post office, of course. Wherever I am, epistolary communication is essential. Kipling's cat and her biro. 'I'm still alive and hoping you are the same.' The editing of life's copy goes on relentlessly. And odd things happen. I once received a postcard of Stockholm which had been posted in London. It was addressed to Ida Jane Evans of Muskugee, Oklahoma. How it landed in the Peloponnese is an unfathomable mystery, but then I once received a letter which was posted in Melbourne and arrived at the village via Vancouver. Of course I posted the Oklahoma letter on to Ida Jane.

Postcards invariably go to Paul in Melbourne because he sends me postcards, usually written during his dinner parties. Between courses. I get letters, too. Once there was a gap of some months, but eventually a letter came in which I was invited to take my pick of the following excuses and then forgive the silence:

1. He'd been kidnapped by a troop of marauding wombats and kept prisoner in their burrow.
2. He'd been bitten by a tsetse fly and had been asleep for months on end.
3. Michelle Pfeiffer had decided she couldn't live without him and had him kept locked up as her plaything for six months.

Of course I forgave him.

Paul and I met when we were seven. We were in the same class at our country school; his parents knew my parents. That skinny, freckled redhead evolved into a bearded *bon viveur* with an eclectic taste in music: he enjoys the occasional stint as a DJ for a provincial radio station. One afternoon a woman rang up and said that the world was going to end at a certain time. When that time came Paul made sure he had a Neville Brothers record playing, because he was sure that the world could not end when the Nevs were on the air. And sure enough, he was right.

Years ago, Paul gave me a vast number of music tapes. As he is one of my links with the past, it is appropriate that many of these tapes recall my mother and father as they were. It is my father's pleasant tenor, for example, that I seem to hear warbling 'Some Enchanted Evening', and one line from 'Just Walkin' In The Rain' is enough to evoke my mother pausing in her housework to listen to the song on the wireless and then saying, 'Ooh, I love you, Johnny Ray.'

But Paul is also very much part of my present and so relishes hearing how my children give me a hard time whenever I try to listen to such archival material. They manage to cope with Johnny Cash keeping a close watch on his heart and thus walking the line, and can understand my listening to Fats Domino, because they know I want to be a wheel some day, but lyrics which rhyme tweedly dum and bubblegum have little attraction. They flee the house when Pat Boone is singing and loud groans greet my favourite, Guy Mitchell. Of course I fight back gamely: 'What on earth is the matter with "Pittsburgh, Pennsylvania?"

I protest. 'Lines about peaches, honey and money have got sex, poetry and exploitation. Life, in a word. And it's got a catchy tune. What more do you want?'

'Kiss and Heavy Metal,' they reply succinctly.

Back to London in the middle of the night.

Time passes very rapidly when one is ageing and on the move, so I have just time to saunter along Birdcage Walk and listen to the Guards' band playing 'Men of Harlech' and 'Annie Laurie'. I am transported back to childhood by the familiar tunes, but grow up in an instant on seeing a flamboyant type undulating along the pavement; he is what the Greeks call a *pousti*. 'Come along, darling,' he coos to a bundle of fluff attached to a stylish lead. He has, this youngish person, the figure of an under-developed, under-exercised, rail-thin ballet dancer, with long legs, like a couple of pencils, encased in lycra tights. He literally skips and dances with glee when the soldiers begin their march, and flutes to no one in particular, 'I *do* love a man in uniform, girls.'

'Think I'll move,' says a nervous young man standing near me.

And as it is nearly departure time again, even though
it seems as if I have only just arrived, I go off to the
recycling bins at the end of the street and dutifully
begin the ritual of depositing newspapers, bottles and
cans. I am joined by an entertaining chap who sports a
white beard and a ready wit. (What encounters you
have, says my friend Elizabeth, grinning, when I tell
her. She said the same thing when I told her about the
beautiful Afro-Caribbean girl who walked up to me in
the tube station and asked whether I would be interested in Christian meetings, and about the woman
who boomed at me in a lift, 'Are you a teacher?' When
I whispered yes, she boomed again, 'I thought so; you
have that look.' What, I wondered, was that look?) The
bearded chap swings off his bike and proceeds to
offload his bottles and papers. He tips his flat cap and
says in the mandatory cut-glass accent, 'Ah, madam, at
least you and I are doing our bit.'

We launch into an easy discussion about ecology,

the state of the environment and the dire ways of politicians, and I think, not for the first time, how easy it is to feel safe with strangers. Well, with a certain sort of stranger. And how some people never want to progress beyond cautious chit-chat in a crowd, are content to remain strangers forever.

'I wish you would wear a stack hat or a crash helmet,' I say boldly, 'when you ride that thing around these busy streets.'

'Ah, madam, what about freedom, individuality, choice and responsibility?' he asks, sounding much like a philosophy lecturer of unhappy memory. 'Of course the young should wear them.'

'Of course. But surely a certain number of people would be very upset if you came a cropper on a hard road. And think of the cost to the State and the taxpayer.'

'Mustn't be like Australia, madam. That place and seatbelts and stack hats indeed. Big Brother. 1984.' He comes close to making an elegant snort, the kind of noise that used to be written as *Pshaw!* or *Faugh!* a century ago.

He looks waggishly at me and I smile my social

'how charmed I am' smile. Aussie-baiter, do your worst; you will get no reaction from me. I no longer explain, let alone apologise for, my origins. Fairy Maturity has flown in the window and waved her magic wand at last. So I bite my tongue. A migrant always has a short tongue, as the biting is a daily occurrence. 'Must be off,' he announces. 'I wish you well, madam.'

'I wish you well, too,' I reply, 'and please don't fall off.'

The world weeps on Good Friday, the Greek *Megali Paraskevi*, but along with the weeping there is an awful lot of movement. Here I am, back in the place about which I feel so profoundly ambivalent. The elements of culture shock are all here; will I ever get used to Athens airport, the dour customs officials, the packs of stray dogs, the horrendous expense of a lukewarm, rubber-tasting cappuccino, the sight of the armoured vehicle parked outside, the fights in the taxi queue?

But this grey morning, with Homer's rosy fingers of dawn just emerging, a taxi driver is helpful and I am grateful. No chance of a bus, he says, and takes me to the railway station, where I have been precisely twice in my life. My parents, on their visits, always favoured the train, and once looked on in shocked amazement when the woman in charge of catering collected their souvlaki sticks and soft-drink cans and hurled them out of the train window. But that was long ago.

Today I remind myself that I am about to travel on one of the great little railways of the world, one that has been the subject of a television documentary. I remind myself of this again when the train starts, moves twenty metres, and then stops.

But first there is the struggle to find my seat, and even entry into the train resembles the difficult ascent of a mountain. The steps seem specifically designed for giants of seven feet plus, and built to scale so that they can lug their suitcases behind them. By some miracle I do not have a heart attack. Nor, showing great restraint, do I have an apoplectic fit during the mandatory disputes and disagreements about seat numbers. These over, I sink onto a grimy and worn blue velvet seat and notice the pockmarked linoleum, the stained concrete blocks of Athenian suburbia, and the cloudless Attic sky before falling uncomfortably asleep, my therapy of return, a detective novel, lying unopened in my lap.

I wake to a timid tap on my shoulder: it is the conductor, wanting to check my ticket and looking offended at having to touch me. Of course I am a strange sight with my undyed hair, my winter-weight long shorts and my Akubra hat, which is, at this moment, emu feathers drooping, falling over my face. Time to observe my fellow passengers. A student is reading. Two or three women, obviously brainwashed and repressed villagers, I think nastily, have settled in for a protracted session of church-gazing, chapel-spotting and chest-crossing. (This is a full-time occupation for the devout Greek Orthodox.) A middle-aged man, overweight, of course, and with a cast in one eye, chomps on biscuits and his fingernails in turn and manages, somehow, to give the rest of his attention to a crossword puzzle. A bottle-blonde, with black boots, floral skirt and a haughty look, snarls at me because my suitcase, propped in the doorway, has let a breath of fresh air into her cosiness. Cosiness = fetid fug, but then bodily thermostats are another area of cultural misunderstanding.

Praise be, Athens is far behind us and I, for one,

start to sigh over the landscape. If only I could hate
Greece. But how can I? When the dandelions are massing and the olive trees are flashing green and silver,
when the Judas trees are in bloom, purple for Lent,
and when I notice the eucalypts with their silver bark
and pink-tipped foliage? How can I when the train
inches its way across a very narrow viaduct and gives
views the car driver never sees of tiny cars crawling
along a ribbon of asphalt a long way below? Fitted in
between the fear and downright terror are explosions
of joy, awe, something, at the sight of mighty mountains stretching far away, for we have now entered the
Peloponnese, and I can fool myself briefly that I am
going home. What I am really doing is going back.

The journey is from another time and the stations
seem made of some forgotten precursor of Lego bricks.
The station attendants, when there are any, wear red
hats and carry wooden signals. Alongside the line black-
clad women watch over flocks of goats and sheep.

I arrange to get off the train at the village nearest
the one I used to call mine. Of course the train is too
long for the platform so I leap down into hip-high
grass and dry spit against the likely presence of snakes.

The conductor hurls my luggage, always too much luggage, after me, and there I stand, lost yet again, in an olive grove. The birds sing cheerfully while I debate what to do. There is a deserted house near the deserted station and that is all. If it were not for my luggage I could walk the five kilometres. As it is I stand and wait.

Things often go right at the last minute in Greece. The killing part is the worrying and wondering whether this rightness will ever happen. I am in luck: the train has disgorged another passenger and there he stands, very tall, about fifty metres away on the platform proper. (He is wearing a stack hat, a coincidence that amuses me.) We begin hailing each other, and he turns out to be one of G's very numerous nephews. He immediately assumes responsibility for his ageing relative and I pay for the taxi that miraculously appears from nowhere: a small price for such a timely rescue.

Easter passes in a blur. I have experienced so many Greek Easters by now that they all run into each other in my memory. Mass at midnight and the wandering back with a lighted candle in order to ensure blessings and benefits, the making of a smoky sign of the Cross above the doorway, the coping with the clashing of the pagan and the Christian, the firecrackers that give some idea of an artillery barrage, the paschal candles decorated with plastic images of Mickey Mouse and red ribbons advertising Coca-Cola.

At sister-in-law Penelope's on Easter Sunday the swallows are nesting under the eaves as usual, and her globes of cheese, sixteen of them, are hanging under those same eaves in a kind of gently swinging mobile sculpture. The men squabble amiably over the spitted lamb. The babies, the new generation, are very well behaved, and it is amusing to see the young macho men doing their bit with rattles and dummies. This is the first Easter without Yiayia, who is still lying in bed, but seems very far removed from this place and the person she once was.

The routine is the same: too much food and then I dance until I'm ready to drop, and still do not want to return to my own house. I break yet another rule by sitting singing with the men and then take myself off on a solitary tour of the village. I pay a few calls,

feeling myself consoled by company, and am complimented on my red tartan skirt and red top. 'You're
wearing the Easter colour,' says a friend. The colour of
the risen Christ, the colour the Tsar always wore on
Easter Day. Red eggs for Easter, demon-defying red.

Consoled by company. Foreign women are in Greece
most often because of Greek men, and our lives have
taken on a pattern. We are always alone, or nearly
always, the companionate marriage being a Western
romantic ideal unfamiliar to the Greek mind. We are
always waiting for somebody; we are always saying
goodbye; we are always trying to comfort ourselves
with improving thoughts – migratory species are less
aggressive than sedentary ones – we have open minds.
But then we suffer because of our open minds and
curse our middle-class self-doubt, yearning vainly for
the effortless confidence and superiority of the upper
and peasant classes.

Once again I'm in limpet mode. I'm always tearing myself off rocks, knowing that the rocks are quite
glad to get rid of me. I'm nearly always in a state of

peculiar conflict, as we all are. Today, for example, I sit and slit the pages of *I Panagia I Gorgona* to the strains of Handel.

Greeks are like elephants. They never forget, at least not where matters of honour are involved. So Nemesis, long delayed, arrives in the shape of Zoe. She has not forgotten that I have mentioned her name in a piece of writing. Only her first name, and I said nothing bad about her, but her vengeful, self-righteous speech is a parody of John Proctor's in *The Crucible*. That's the drama, and then there are the histrionics, the tongue-lashings, the reproaches to contend with. It is all too much. I am bewildered by the imputation of malice where none was intended, and by the sheer self-confidence, lack of guilt and assumption of the inalienable right of verbal attack. I feel sick to my stomach and burst into uncontrollable tears. 'Stop that,' she commands. 'You're upsetting me.' At the end of this episode she announces that we are friends again, that everything will be as it was before. She is, after all, a devout Christian Orthodox. But my view is that we are not friends, for that is clearly impossible, and nothing between us will ever be the same again.

My children continue to entertain me, even though the house once again reeks of dirty socks and shirts and I make grumbling noises about *eau de garçon* and *parfum de boy*. Jo and I watch a film on television. That is to say, I am quite engrossed while Jo lifts an eye every so often from his essential reading, the weekly basketball magazine.

'Oh, heavens,' I say dramatically.

'What is it?'

'She, the heroine, is breaking the hero's heart.'

'Oh, I thought it was something serious.'

Like his second brother, Jo is cultivating the art of being Mr Cool. 'That Odysseus was a wily character,' I remarked once, during his study of Homer.

'Of course,' came the laconic reply. 'That's why he's so famous.'

When they are all here, the din of loud and high-tension Greek and my inability to get a word in edgewise in either language often tries my patience, so that occasionally I am transformed into what my mother used to call a Billingsgate fishwife.

'Shut up, the lot of you,' I screech, 'or I'll do something drastic.'

'Oh yeah?'

'Oh yeah. I'll play my Baroque Classics tape.'

'No, no. Spare us. Anything but that.' And they guffaw heartily, knowing they are safe. I won't play it because they will yak mercilessly just the same.

Now Tom is here making pronouncements. There are also tales of suicides and armed robberies and an NCO forcing a private to swallow a radio aerial. A dialogue is set up, in which I hear my own voice and its constructions as a kind of echo.

'My room,' he declares, 'is an example of restrained anarchy.'

'Where does the restraint come in?' I ask.

He covers a range of topics from the dreadfulness of the Athenian *nouveau riche* to the almost equal dreadfulness of Australian Rules football.

'What's the matter with Aussie Rules?'

'Now, don't start all that stuff about it being the noblest game on earth.'

'No, I won't, because that's cricket.'

'Oh yeah. Well, Australian Rules doesn't have enough fights, and a bit of blood on the ground and in the outer is always to be desired.'

'It is *not* always to be desired,' I retort, while thinking that things have indeed changed.

'The spectators are always too taciturn. I mean, all they can do is drag the can of Foster's away from their lips long enough to bleat, Ya prick, and that's about it. Not very articulate, is it?' I am forced to agree that it isn't. So then he changes the subject.

'People over the age of fifty shouldn't have sex.'

I cannot let this pass and so I ask carefully, 'Why not?'

'Oh Mum, the sheer droopiness of it all, for God's sake.'

I sniff and say I hope I'm still around on his fiftieth birthday. Or better still, on his sixtieth.

I discover that Jo, too, is being groomed for a career in the Greek army. I am horrified and upset, rebellious and wounded: my children have been misappropriated.

'Calm down,' says Tom, sipping a weak ouzo, puffing on a strong cigarette and stretching his very long legs, thus making the living room look like an obstacle course. 'Just think. You'll have your two officer pillars of society and me, your bohemian scholar of the arts.'

Damn his eyes. He always makes me laugh, has a unique capacity to rescue me from the depths of my melancholy.

'The arts being those of nightclubbing and playing computer games, I take it?'

Lunch by the beach. My companion and I (I'm going to take up food journalism once I can summon up enough interest in food) eat and drink and natter away and then become mesmerised by the sight of a tip-truck carrying a load of sand. It backs into the beach-restaurant area and dumps its load. We watch with great enjoyment as the tailboard falls off almost immediately and is then buried under a neat heap of grey. The driver emerges from the cabin, notices something is missing, scratches his head, grabs a spade that just happens to be lying nearby, and proceeds to dig the tailboard out.

The job has taken at least twice as long as it should have done: in Greece time is no object.

A neighbour boasts of how she has persuaded Yiayia to drink her milk. 'I told her that our All Holy Lady would be very angry with her if she didn't drink up,' she says complacently.

I, for one, wish that our All Holy Lady, rather than scolding Yiayia, would simply tell her to pack it in, to give up this long struggle which can have only one outcome. But I bite my tongue. Again.

The month nears its end with Anzac Day. Time to fly the flag again and I remember another Anzac Day in Australia, and the sign at Oakleigh station, Melbourne, chalked in clumsy capitals on a small blackboard: 'ALL DIGGERS WEARING MEDALS TO TRAVEL FREE TODAY. GOOD ON YA, DIGS!' Today a parcel of Anzac biscuits, wrapped in aluminium foil, arrives from Melbourne. At least someone loves us.

This same weekend Tom, now back in Athens, rings

to say that he is to spend forty-eight hours on duty at a deserted fort, where the population consists solely of rats, feral cats, a few Albanians of the illegal immigrant type, and a witch who cackles. There is some variety in the life of a national serviceman, it seems. Recently he was part of a squad which had to go to a church in order to present arms to a miraculous icon of Our Lady. The policemen were their usual brutish selves and had a high old time pushing and shoving the crowds of devout old women whose only wish was to light a candle and to kiss the face of the Mother of God.

I wait at the bus stop, on my way to Kalamata yet again. A blue cart, drawn by a tiny donkey, approaches. The animal is wearing blinkers made out of large pieces of rubber tyre and held on by twine. He stops and is given a sound whipping by his master. He tosses his head, shows his teeth and staggers on. The bell on his harness chinks, and the fragment of red rug tied to the back of the cart flutters in the spring breeze.

An Alfa Romeo whizzes past in the opposite direction and I think, not for the first time, how appropriate it is that the Greeks invented the word 'anachronism'. Different eras collide here regularly: I am still not really accustomed to the sight of priests driving cars and carrying supermarket bags. And now I notice that the poorest of Albanian labourers are using mobile phones compulsively, as are, I'm told, Venetian gondoliers.

During the bus trip I am unexpectedly taken to an area I have never visited before. Suddenly I see what can only be described as a carnation farm: the rows of scarlet, pink and white march up and down sloping hillsides. At night I dream of tearing along on a bike which has no steering mechanism.

Portents of summer: there is a salamander in the sink and a mouse in the outside stair cupboard. In last summer's notebook I find the following list:

1. An ant plague. (Swarms on every surface, honey jars having to be stood in bowls of water, all that.)

2. A snake in the garden.

3. Two dead birds upstairs.

4. Mosquitoes galore (normal). The size of small aeroplanes (also normal).

5. Two rats, one shot in the bathroom after I'd cleaned it. The bathroom, that is.

6. A cockroach in the bath (and God knows where else, there are whole colonies of this prehistoric monster).

7. A tick in my toe. (I stupidly tore it out and tore out a whole lump of flesh as well, slow learner me.)

Ah, the hierarchy of suffering. 'You've never had all *that*, Elizabeth,' I say, when back in England. 'No,' she replies, no ruffles on that calm surface, 'only scorpions in our beds in France.'

M A Y

May Day, and G makes a wreath, a custom that was never mine, one that failed to survive the long journeys from Europe to Australia.

Ozzie and I go for a walk, up into the mountains where yellow gorse is making a spiky, jigsaw pattern, where patches of light form and dissolve as dark clouds move and shift overhead. Virginia stock is growing wild in banks of pink and purple.

In the village itself the Smyrna veteran, the only one left from the battles of 1922, is still tottering up and down the street at regular intervals. The barber who seldom cuts hair sits in the spring sunshine and has an early lunch or late breakfast of bread and tomato, both hacked at with a pocket-knife. Two young things who mind shops into which people rarely go sit on window-sills and swing their legs in a fashion their *yiayiathes* would heartily disapprove of. Their *yiayiathes* would not approve of them sending fan letters to Johnny Depp and Tom Cruise, either, which is what I observe in the post office one day.

Two old friends of the philhellene variety come to call. We go to watch Jo play volleyball and then we sit and spin a long thread of gossip throughout the rest of the day: marriage and politics and Melbourne and Greece, the different fibres of reality forming some sort of pattern, as they have done since we met in 1981.

They are not surprised to hear the latest offering from the hairdressing salon. Panayota informs me that a new church is being erected in a remote spot by a young man who is totally unskilled in the building arts, the olive harvest being his main area of expertise. But the church is nearly finished, St George having told this devout artisan all he needs to know. The saint is taking care of everything, so that the builder, also named George, is not at all worried about the lack of an icon. When the saint is ready the icon will appear. Panayota tells me this last with an air of complete certainty. This is an accepted fact, the icon's arrival. I am deeply, deeply envious of her faith.

Fighting the demons this week: an over-active imagination and a tendency to melancholy are not a desirable combination. A blanket of despair descends and settles for various reasons. One of these is that I am not a very satisfactory historian and tend to misinterpret evidence, and so persuade myself of an imminent change of heart in other people. Alas, the hearts I know do not change, and why I ever thought they were capable of it I have no idea. Shocking egotism it is, I suppose, to consider, even for a moment, that I am worth changing for.

And of course the sense of being doubly displaced never goes away. I remember a Frenchman, an academic, summing this whole issue up very neatly for me. He wrote to tell me, 'Once exchanged, forever estranged.'

Mick is here, quietly excited by the fact that he is now a commando sergeant in the Greek SAS. Needless to say, I am not at all excited. He sits in the sunshine peacefully sewing his flashes and badges on sundry shirts and jackets, while I pray that no sister-in-law comes to call, for what he is doing is undoubtedly mothers' work. Later he walks around the house with a dripping green beret on his head. 'Just getting it into the right shape,' he says by way of explanation, and goes on to tell me of his latest adventure as part of a squad sent to subdue a crowd of anarchists who had been rioting outside a rock concert.

He has taken up kick-boxing, of all philistine pas-times. 'Couldn't you have taken up the violin instead?' I ask plaintively but foolishly, to the accompaniment of raucous laughter. 'If you can't beat them, join them' has always been one of my mottoes so I request a lesson, which ensues promptly. We make a strange sight with our prancing and weaving. I am puffing like a grampus within two minutes, and devoutly hope Mick cannot hear my bones creaking and cracking under the unaccustomed strain. He probably can. Every now and then I fear one of my bones will snap, given that I am in my sunset years and doubtless osteoporotic: I make a mental note to eat more sardines, even as Mick is saying, 'Could've smashed your right jaw in just then,' in a very matter-of-fact fashion.

In between times, he is very informative on the subject of magic in rural Greece, and regales me with tales about witches and warlocks: I hadn't realised that a village acquaintance had consulted a warlock when she feared that the whole family had been put under a spell. Presumably the warlock reassured her and accomplished what the passage of time would have done anyway. Not even a spell can last forever, in spite of what the fairytales suggest, but preventative measures are a good idea. One of these, Mick informed me solemnly, consists in young men being constantly on their guard: on no account must a Samson allow any would-be Delilah to gain possession of a lock of his hair. He himself, thanks to the Greek army and its regulations, has no locks to speak of.

Tom rings from Athens to say that his new colonel is making his life miserable. But, I say, isn't that what colonels are for?

Jo refuses to go to the raw young barber. 'My ears,' he says. 'I do not want to risk my anatomy.'

The arrival of the copy-edit of *A Stranger Here* arrives and has the salutary effect of rousing me from gloom. A week later, an exhausted heap from the effects of checking and rechecking, I take the precious bundle to the courier's office in Kalamata, where a very pleasant young man drives me mad by his refusal to let me complete a sentence. I struggle through the ordeal of packaging and labelling and then realise he is delicately asking me whether there is anything of a pornographic nature in the parcel. 'We have laws against pornography in Greece,' he announces.

'I know,' I reply, and do not add that I also know that they are honoured more in the breach than in the observance. I become jocular, a bad habit, but also a defence mechanism. 'Alas, no,' I say. 'Bad luck about that. If I knew how to write pornography I would be a lot, lot richer than I am now.' He turns big shocked brown eyes upon me. Surely a female as old as I should not say such things? But then I am clearly foreign, so what can one expect?

Finances being in a frightening state, I take myself off to a teaching job at a language school which runs both morning and evening classes. Such jobs are easily come by, as mine is still the only Australian accent in town. (The Greek-Australian accent is quite different, at least to my experienced ear.) My teenage students are lively and pleasant, the work familiar, and there is a whole world of entertainment outside the school window. Tom once spent an entire term looking at a woman who wore a black bikini and sat out on her balcony every night she knew the school was operating. Education comes in various guises.

Today a fat old woman sweeps and mops her balcony. She wears the traditional morning garb of the suburban housewife: a shapeless floral housecoat. A cigarette dangles from the corner of her mouth as she sloshes water from the balcony onto the street below. She and her ilk are tough types, winners in the battle Greeks call the *biopali*, literally translated as the struggle of life. Long years of very hard work have resulted in the reward of a little flat in town, the pleasure of taps and running water. Drawing water from wells is often the hardest work of all, and is the most basic.

In the village my ancient neighbours, dressed in dusty black dresses and aprons, straw hats anchored with white elastic over their headscarves, bend up and down in sweeping movements all morning, gleaning, using sickles to remove the tall stalks of grass that the plough-man has missed. They are doing what they have always done, getting ready for the planting of summer vege-tables and crops. Are they never bored? I ask myself, not for the first time, and ponder yet again the fatalism and lack of curiosity that are so much a part of peasant life. Curiosity is a luxury that a peasant cannot afford.

Working with people whose second language is English helps me approach my first from a new angle. In a practice interview a student solemnly informs me that she knows a man 'made from velvet'. 'Do you really?' I ask her. 'Where can *I* find one?'

In the busy pre-examination week another student wails, 'What's going to happen to me when I have a strange examiner? You're like my mother.' As her mother has the reputation of being an arrogant nitwit, I am not too pleased, but can see what she means.

Foreign wives. Justine comes to call, looking older and much sadder. Her husband has become a believer: he and the marriage are saved. Oh yes? I say, hoping my deeply felt cynicism does not show. Won't I come to prayer meetings? she asks. When I say I'll think about it — my insincere way of announcing *absolutely not* — she looks so wounded that I rush to explain that my grandmothers put me off all that, and that seeing foreign women enduring does me no good at all, as I am fed up with endurance and fortitude, having tried both to very little avail.

At least Justine's husband has been prepared to listen and to take some sort of action. At gatherings of foreign wives my American friend Sandy waxes eloquent on this subject from time to time.

'Most of these guys expect to present themselves at the Pearly Gates sooner or later. Later, they hope, I guess, but when they get there old St Peter's gonna ask them for an account of themselves and their treatment of their wives. And they're gonna say things like "I didn't drink. Well, not a lot. I didn't stay out late. Well, only three or four times a week. And I didn't beat her. And I didn't upset the children or criticise her cooking." And do you know what old St Peter's going to say?'

'No,' we chorus, as we are expected to do.

'He's gonna say, bless his old heart, "Well, gee, guys, tell me what you *did* do!" Tell me now, am I right, or am I not?'

'Of course you're right,' we chorus again, because we believe in accentuating the positive and because we are tired of sins of omission.

Now I, for one, want change, revolution if necessary. Above all, I want peace of mind, and I don't think my attendance at prayer meetings in a foreign country is going to produce it.

Justine goes on to instruct me gently about religion at different stages of life. In youth we are influenced by others, clearly, but in maturity we take on religion for our own sake and on our own terms. 'I'm not an atheist,' I tell her truthfully. 'I pray: I pray for my children and for my friends.'

'You should pray for yourself,' she says, smiling the wistful smile of disappointment.

'Oh, I do,' I reply, and do not add that I cannot bear the continuing silence which seems to be the only answer I ever receive. My fault, I imagine. Perhaps I am not listening in the right way, am turning a deaf ear to divine advice I do not want or feel unable to follow.

G moans that nobody follows his advice, in this case that animals are for work. Jo collects cats – he always has done – so that G feels he is running a feline Salvation Army centre. The latest acquisitions are Jam, so-called because of his apricot colour, and Rasputin, an extremely aloof and aristocratic Russian Blue whose official home is with a retired couple who live a short distance away. Jo gives both animals saucers of milk and kitchen scraps when nobody is looking, so that they are becoming rotund of body and complacent of demeanour.

Attitudes towards animals produce more cross-cultural tension. G's uncle, a man I dearly loved, was in the habit of hobbling his donkey with a length of wire buried as far as it would go into the animal's right foreleg. The poor creature had, not surprisingly, a tendency to bite, and so was muzzled by an arrangement of chicken wire. Years ago, an old peasant of my acquaintance tried to bury his ancient donkey alive, and was very annoyed when the beast managed to stagger out of its premature grave. I have seen a donkey with both ears cut off: the resultant holes gaped pathetically, and persistent Peloponnesian flies made the animal's life a misery. His tail worked overtime, to not much effect. At least G contents himself with directing a token kick, which never connects, in the direction of Jam and Rasputin whenever he leaves the house.

And surely moderation is the thing. An Englishman living in rural Greece once returned home to find that his goat had strangled itself on her tether. Immediately he set about giving his pet mouth-to-mouth resuscitation. To no avail. I later learned of an Englishwoman who had carried out the same act successfully. On her tortoise. She had also, when occasion demanded, given the reptile an enema. Once you start hearing these stories you hear more. Mick's army friend had an armadillo for a pet. It was a smallish one, apparently, which was just as well, seeing that it inhabited the back bedroom of an Athenian flat. And then there is the young American woman of my acquaintance who keeps an iguana in her South Kensington flat. When she bought him he fitted into the palm of her hand; now he is over a hundred and twenty centimetres long and spends a lot of time in the bath.

Thinking of Jo and his cats triggers more memories of my mother. She and my father, who had befriended a banana-addicted monkey in Borneo during the war, were very tolerant of pets of all sorts: guinea pigs, white mice, budgerigars, newts in jars, and always a dog or two. A cat followed Mum home from choir practice once and never went away, so we had to get another to keep it company. This was the pattern of the years.

Another pattern formed around music and singing. Both my mother and her mother-in-law, on whom she doted, belonged to church choirs and Country Women's Association choirs. My mother had a very clear soprano, my grandmother a rich contralto. My mother's favourites were 'My Task' and 'Bless This House'; my grandmother's 'The Londonderry Air' and 'The Holy City'. Both women were conscientious about practising, sometimes alone, sometimes together, so that my sister and I were forever humming snatches of serious anthems, were constantly lifting our eyes and remembering the name of the Lord rather than trusting in chariots and horses. As for princes, we never thought they were to be trusted at all, but we knew that the Lord was Alpha and Omega because He Himself said so. For light entertainment we gathered lilacs in the spring again, and felt reassured by the promise that there would be bluebirds over the White Cliffs of Dover.

When Mum wasn't practising she would sing the old songs that had been sung to her: singing round the piano was an almost nightly occurrence. Nothing was ever explained. We did not realise, for example, that the bluebirds had been flapping about in their appointed place for a considerable time. When we sang 'My Pretty Jane', I was puzzled because the moon was on the rye and the corn was in the ear. Whose? And how uncomfortable. We lived for years in a flat, dusty township in the hot Wimmera and sang lilting melodies as each summer night gasped to an exhausted close; the songs told of green mountains and pure crystal fountains, the sun declining beneath the blue sea, the beautiful vale of Tralee – wherever and whatever that was – and of the cool shades of evening, and all these things were strictly irrelevant.

It didn't matter. All that mattered then was the pleasure. All that matters now is the clutch of grief I feel whenever I hear any part of these dozens of songs from England, Ireland and Scotland, for now my sister, too, is dead. I have no daughter, so that the feminine solidarity, established so early and taken so much for granted, has gone forever. Mothers and daughters – that tug of love, the tie that never quite breaks, despite the endless absence.

A much older friend of mine once spent a long time in hospital. Her mother had been dead for thirty years, but as she lay miserably while the nurses tried to tempt her jaded appetite, all she wanted was her mother's afternoon-tea bread and butter. Sliced very thin, just the way her mother always made it.

On May the 29th I go on my daily trip to the post office, pass two or three teenagers on the threshold, and find postmaster Theo caught between sorrow and anger. Anger seems to be in the ascendant. 'Would you believe,' he says, shaking his head, 'that that lot does not know what day it is?'

It is still quite early; I try to remember what day it is.

'Of course today's not Tuesday,' he mutters, and suddenly I have it. The City. Constantinople fell to the Ottoman Turks on Tuesday, May the 29th, 1453, and that day in particular, and Tuesdays in general, have remained days of ill omen in the Greek world ever since. I make sympathetic noises. Because I am not from the same background I cannot feel his emotion, but I feel his bewilderment: why does this generation not know, when generations spanning five hundred years knew only too well?

Whenever one or other of my boys refused to eat, Yiayia used to say, 'You must eat your vegetables. Otherwise, how are you going to grow to be a big man and take the City?' Theo's illiterate grandmother knew more about the fall of Constantinople, its consequences and its effect on the Greek consciousness, than today's school children do.

Theo is a worried man. '*Pou vriskomaste?* Where are we? *Pou parme?* Where are we going?' he asks me. I have no answers.

JUNE

Thought for the month: people do not change, they simply become more of what they are. Which leads me to consider various attitudes to life, my own especially. Rightly or wrongly, I've never been able to refrain from tasting when the wine cup glistens, have always been ready to look on beauty's charming, and have never had a hope of stopping my ear against a good singer, or speaker for that matter. Voices are so important. This easy-living-and-quiet-dying bit is clearly not for me, and the coffin lid had better be good and strong because I'll be pounding and kicking even while the nails are going in. And probably afterwards as well. I hate the thought of missing out on anything and of having a whole lot of questions unanswered. And nothing happens in the grave; not even ordinary things.

I glance out the window and see a cat in the act of pouncing on something. Oh God, a bird. But no, it is a small lizard. Through the glass the cat gazes at me defiantly with the body in its mouth: the palely orange underside glints in the sun of midday. 'Oh Mum,' says Jo, seeing me wince, 'it's only a lizard.'

Once again a lost week: there seem to be an awful lot of them in Greece, but perhaps there are just an awful lot of them in life. During this week Yiayia started to refuse to eat, and now she has taken a sudden turn for the worse, although her 'bad' has often been bad enough. The doctor has been and has given her twelve hours to live, although he did add the rider that he is not God. Well, she always was stubborn, and now thirty-six hours have passed.

Her favourite son has taken it upon himself to organise the administration of antibiotic injections.

Of course, once he has given the order he has nothing to do with the practicalities, not even staying around to see the first injection go in. I was sitting on the end of the bed, praying Yiayia would die from the shock. The needle must have gone into the bone as she has virtually no flesh left. The nurse and Yiayia's daughters are very disapproving, but powerless to act against masculine authority. At least so far.

Selfishly, I want Yiayia to die before I leave for London. If she dies while I'm waiting at the bus stop, I'll kill her. In the meantime, she lies flat on her back with her headscarf still on. Last night there were fourteen women in her room and twenty-four men outside in the courtyard. A social occasion, of course. In the room, before the visitors came, the family engaged in much noisy discussion of arrangements and plans. Burials have to take place very quickly in Greece, but even so I wondered fearfully whether Yiayia could actually hear them all disputing and giving their opinions, and if so, what must it be like.

'*Don't* put all this in a book,' ordered Zoe. I rolled my eyes and thought, Hmm, not a bad idea. But I will never permit a Greek translation. Zoe is now all sweetness and light, in a sort of cathartic glow, and I play along with this, while continually longing to kick her wide shins to a pulp.

During the vigil old women feel free to totter over to the deathbed, draw back the sheet and check on the state of Yiayia's hands and feet. Theories are expounded as to her colour, the shape of her jaw, and so on. I sit there, ears flapping, learning all the time, and thinking guiltily what parasites and cannibals writers are. One of my grandmothers, I recall suddenly, was able to lay bodies out. Not a skill I have, not one I aspire to having.

The eldest daughter at last finds the courage to defy her brother and forbid further injections. 'Did I do the right thing?' she asks, seeking my opinion for the first time in nearly twenty years. 'Absolutely,' I reply.

So now Yiayia lies breathing stertorously, mouth open. Her O of a mouth and her sunken jaws are like a parody of Munch's *Scream*, surely parodic enough in itself. She is now a woman almost totally reduced, barely recognisable. In this hot June, ants crawl in her eyes before anyone notices.

A long afternoon passes, punctuated only by Yiayia's irregular breathing and the quiet exchange of chatter between her daughters and me. Death, like birth, is women's business but I am not quite sure why I am here, just that some instinct is driving me. I did not see my mother die; only an anonymous pastoral-care worker was with her at the end, and I feel guilty about that.

The suspense: several times we think Yiayia has breathed her last. When she does stop breathing and we are sure, action is the thing, much to my amazement. There is also confusion. My sister-in-law expertly binds her mother's jaw with the strip of white linen which has been kept in readiness, but does not know what to do next. Brother-in-law arrives with a saucepan full of wine for the ritual washing of the body, and suddenly the knowledgeable neighbours appear and start their work. The youngest daughter cannot bear to watch, but my curiosity overcomes me, and, after all, there is little connection between my passionate, cantankerous *pethera* and the shrunken, putty-coloured little form lying naked on the bed and being handled none too gently by the women.

Eventually Yiayia is dressed for her *teleftaio taxithi*,

her last journey, dressed, I note to my surprise, in navy-blue rather than the black which is all she has worn for as long as I have known her. Her costume is complete: gloves, shoes and headscarf. Later she is taken upstairs to the *sala*, the best room, where she lies in a coffin ornately carved with the double-headed eagle of Byzantium. Her shroud is covered in red and pink carnations, candles burn at her head and feet, and before her head is covered at sunset we all have a sighting of the brief and strange transforming beauty of death, which enables those left behind to have a glimpse of youth, to store a memory of the person the deceased has been.

I put on my black dress and join my sisters-in-law for part of the all-night vigil. I hold the hand of one while she sobs and voices a cry as old as time: the cry, the lament, for home. 'The house will be locked up. What will happen to our lives? What will happen to our memories? This is the end of everything.' I try to tell her that I understand, but I think she has no idea of how I, of all people, comprehend the loss of home only too keenly. (Next day Jo, before the funeral, asks, 'What will happen to the house now?' The house is, after all, a part of him. He was conceived in the room in which his father was born. This is a loss which moves him slowly but inexorably towards the end of his youth. It seems to me that it was her youth, as well as her mother and her home, that Jo's aunt had mourned during the night.)

As I predicted, I have no hope of enduring the all-night vigil. When I leave, everybody is satisfied: I have attended but will get some sleep. The other women nod virtuously as I leave, feeling superior in strength and duty. They know they have pleased God.

Next morning there is an oppressive, exhausted silence in the room. Yiayia's head is uncovered again and a cross of white flowers has been placed among the red and pink carnations.

Three priests arrive and say prayers over the body; the eldest daughter places a hand on her mother's head and asks tenderly, but using the formal, second-person plural, the ritual question, '*Pou pate?*' Where are you going? The answer is both obvious and not obvious.

Practically the whole village accompanies the hearse to the church. This village is her place: her father and husband were both priests here, so that etiquette, apart from any other consideration, demands that people attend. Jo, carrying one of many enormous wreaths on poles, walks with his cousins in front of the hearse. His brothers have been unable to get leave. The wreaths are made of red and white chrysanthemums, and now Yiayia's coffin is borne slowly across what, as late as the 1820s, used to be a plain where lavender grew wild. So reported the English traveller W. M. Leake, who published his famous *Travels in the Morea* in 1830.

G has always had a tendency to faint, and this worry nags at me all the way to the church and through the service. He manages to stay upright, but his younger brother breaks down completely at one stage and seeks solace, not in the arms of his wife, but in those of his brothers and nephews. And I ask myself bitterly, once again, Where do women *fit* in this society, and what are they for?

At some stage I register everything: the ritual, the dip and soar of the choristers' voices, the impression of the message 'I am the Light of the World' taking on reality as every person in the congregation lights a candle and snuffs it out at a certain point in the ceremony. Through a cloud of incense I see Jo biting his fingernails. I also see the glitter of tears in his eyes.

And then I, too, weep: the other daughters-in-law do not shed a tear. 'She's a good girl, but weepy,' my grandmother said of her daughter-in-law, my mother. It seems I am much the same. But I am not crying for Aphrodite, not really. She was eighty-eight and had lived quite long enough. I weep because of the inevitability of change, for the fact that she has been a presence in my life for thirty-one years; I weep out of a sense of waste and of vain regret, for the futility of our antagonisms. I weep for what might have been because the conflict seems to me, and always did seem, to have been quite unnecessary. I weep because I want to be a child again, and in this desolation want to be comforted by my own mother, and because neither of these things can ever be. Childhood has gone forever, my mother is dead, and there is no one to comfort me.

Weeks later in London I make the acquaintance of an ex-policeman who tells me how he once had to break into a house because the next-door neighbour suspected that the old woman inhabitant had died. This turned out to be indeed the case. The woman's son came and while the police were still there left a note for the milkman: 'No more milk.' 'I've always wanted to write a play about that phrase,' the ex-policeman told me awkwardly, 'but I don't know how.'

I have learned, rather painfully, not to say too much in England, where most people are so wary of the slightest emotional intrusion, but I longed to tell him how right his impulse was, how accurate his feelings were to be moved by that mundane gesture, by the thought that all our striving, passion and pain comes down to this: no more milk, no more anything.

Recent events seem to concentrate all their intensity into these last few minutes at the bus stop. I am waiting to catch the bus to Athens and then the plane to London. The company of one is, as usual, silent, the quietness that reverberates cacophonous. I attempt my usual jocularity as a weapon against the pain of saying goodbye to Jo, who has gone off with his mates, and I wonder, also as usual, why I bother, since there is never any response. The bitterness of departure is upon me. I stand under the gum trees and know there are none where I am going. Nor are there any jacarandas with their purple bells, no Smyrna acacias with their parasol shapes and feathery fronds of pink and yellow, certainly no bottlebrushes bristling with scarlet, and why I am suddenly obsessed by trees I cannot imagine. Except that they are symbols of that very elusive concept, home.

Roots seem to be a common preoccupation. But I happen, long after my latest departure, to read the words of Theodore Zeldin quite by chance, and learn that my botany and that of most people is out of date. He maintains that leaves are just as important, an idea which has never really occurred to me, but now comes as a blessed relief. I must keep reminding myself of it:

A generation which values adaptability as much as tradition, which seeks energy and creativity and openness of mind, must like the idea of drinking in the light of the sun, from whatever direction it shines. The smell of the air becomes sweeter when roots produce leaves, which make it possible for other forms of life to exist. Applied to humans, this means that it is not just where they come from that

matters, but where they are going, what kind of curiosity
or imagination they have, and how they use it, both by day
and by night.

The fickle finger of Fate. The small world of the
Peloponnese. Once in the bus I find myself seated
behind G's first cousin and his wife, who live in a village
about fifteen kilometres away and are very traditional,
have no car, live very modestly and turn up, flying the
flag, as it were, at funerals. I am still wearing deep black
and the woman shows a hesitant recognition, for they
attended Yiayia's funeral only ten days ago. I am wearing
dark glasses and feeling numb and so look away.

When the bus stops for the lunch break, I have a
pang of conscience and introduce myself. And of
course they are courteous, charming and chatty, he
more than she. Back in the bus I long to take a photo
of her brown hands with their crinkled walnut surface as they pat and adjust the short plait which she
wears twisted up the back of her head. They are a
testimony to a lifetime's work, with lines and cracks
stained with Greek earth, the *homa elliniko* that

countless generations of migrants have yearned over. She was the woman who, years ago, broke the chicken's neck in the courtyard and served the departed piece of poultry up to us two hours later.

I work out that this couple has been married forty years, and am envious of the ease with which they sit beside each other, comfortably touching and in touch. They have retained that most important quality – curiosity. No siesta or nodding off for them: they look at their Peloponnesian countryside, theirs, that landscape that so wrenches my heart, and do not miss anything. They chat, converse, and point out this and that. Theirs is a supremely comfortable communication, greatly to be envied.

The old question is asked: Which is better, Greece or Australia? I shrug helplessly, feeling that there is no answer, for at this stage of my life I am blindly attached to both, and am now on my way to London, that long, long umbilical cord, more twisted and knotted and pulsing with life for me than anyone can guess. I tell them where I am going, and they wish me *kalo taxithi*, bon voyage, but cannot comprehend. The shutter drops, for they will never travel further than Athens, where their son has a shop. Briefly, I envy them their certainties, their boundaries, their expectations.

They are, above all, natural. She does not wear make-up and never has, and it is quite obvious that neither of them ever goes to a dentist. Safe in their received lives which they have never dreamed of altering, they will die contented and guiltless. Privileged. They have done what was expected of them, have done their duty, are probably cautiously sure of a better life beyond the grave. It also seems to me that they have been, and still are, happy.

Zeldin again. He quotes Girolamo Cardano (1501–76), who said, 'It makes for happiness to be what you can, when you cannot be what you would.' I must keep reminding myself of that, too. And try to forget William Drummond (1585–1649), who wrote, 'What served it to be happy so?'

Taxi drivers in Athens. Well, I've written about them before. This particular one is huge and hugely unattractive, but still possessed of that unassailable self-confidence and unquenchable vitality so much a part of the Greek heritage. I feel my red corpuscles fading to pale pink by the minute. The driver is the soul of manipulative courtesy, so of course he picks up other passengers en route, a practice which is illegal, takes me miles out of my way, moans politely about the length of my journey, but at least heaves my bags out of the boot while insincerely worrying about leaving me alone and unmet in the heat. This worry allows him to ignore, very adroitly, his obligation to give me change out of a 5000-drachma note. Shall I kiss you? he beams, and I hope he does not see me give an involuntary shudder. All this ambiguous familiarity is because he comes from a village, his *patritha*, only about ten kilometres away from the one I have just left.

London taxi drivers invariably ask, 'Where to, darling?' If I am wearing my Akubra hat they don't bother to ask, so that I have to tell them that, no thank you, I am *not* going to Earl's Court. Not today, anyway. Once the journey is begun a tactful and very British silence usually follows, but on one memorable occasion the driver, a man in his sixties, had a taste for my kind of music. 'Anything Goes' was playing on the car radio. We started humming together in a slightly inhibited fashion. By the time we reached Belsize Park we were singing along: the last number, I recall, was 'You're Sixteen, You're Beautiful, and You're Mine'. I paid the fare; we gave each other sheepish looks and then laughed companionably. There are some advantages to ageing, after all.

To the large Athenian house, beautiful garden and warm hospitality which will envelop me for a night. I am not good company at this time, although the sense of freedom and relief is starting. It bothers me that I am so materialistic in my late middle-age, but I love this huge house with its planned, *conscious* garden, and its drought-resistant plants. (I plant pansies in the Peloponnese, for God's sake.) There is a sense of tradition as well: the embroideries, the hand-woven curtains, and culture in the form of piano, violin, books, paintings, prints and ornaments.

Talk, talk, talk: I am like a sponge, one that has been dry and brittle for ever but is now starting to fill and expand and feel more comfortable because of it, more the way a sponge should feel. I pack my black clothes in my suitcase and set off for London in bright colours.

July

I barely have time to catch my breath in London before I set off to Wales, that place which Dr Johnson opined 'offered nothing to the speculation of the traveller'. 'Cardiff,' says a friend. 'Hmm. *Not* one of the world's great capitals.'

As it is, the place makes little impression on me; I am there to meet people, namely my father, who is on holiday, having started a new life some time ago. Old people can often do this, it seems to me, while it is the middle-aged who get stuck in the transitional process. I, for example, seem unwillingly glued to my old life, in spite of my efforts with various solvents, assiduously applied. But parts of my very old life have disappeared, places and people, and I sit in the train and think of bubbles of time which seal themselves off and float away, never to return.

When I look at the map of Britain Cardiff seems very far off. I may well fall off the edge after what I think will be a very long journey. In fact my geography is so appalling, and my sense of distance so geared to the southern hemisphere, that I cannot believe it when the train arrives after only two hours.

Wet weather. How green are the valleys, and no wonder. When I was a child I had no idea that such lushness could possibly exist. My father used to bang the rungs of the rainwater tank at the start of every summer and turn away grimly. We knew then that if the notoriously fickle stormclouds did not deliver, the earth would harden over the months and come to resemble cracked china, that the garden would wither, the lawn turn to dust, and that we would go unwashed for days at a time. In the upper part of the Greek village the wells run dry in a bad summer, and water tankers grind their way up the mountainside every afternoon.

Later I learn about Wales and water, about holy wells and the power of water to heal. Dragons were said to fight beneath a great lake; the lord of the land

was imprisoned in a waterfall. In ancient Wales dragons lived beside men and often had to be slaughtered
so that princesses could be rescued. I can believe in
dragons easily enough, even in waterless Greece, but
find it much harder to believe in princesses and impossible to believe in rescue.

I go down a coal mine. Many of my ancestors were
miners, miners of tin, copper and gold, so that I have
conscientiously been down mines on both sides of the
world. These mines, of course, are tourist attractions,
but I cannot feel myself a tourist. The sensations of
being underground are dreadful. All that weight, all
that thickness is no longer a protection, and the notion
of it is only a part of the horror. There's the seeping
cold and the darkness, the dampness, and the air which
is not as air should be. The nagging thoughts of shocking accidents which occurred so easily in the past, and
the equally shocking facts of history: in Cornwall children were sometimes sent down mines for three days
at a time. I have gazed in a kind of fascinated repulsion
at television film of those conveyor-belt arrangements
which in America and South Africa take men literally
into the bowels of the earth, so aptly named, so black

and dirty, tucked and creased as they are – these shafts, tunnels and passages – so dank, so full of toxins, so likely to explode, be blocked or collapse at any moment, so literally and metaphorically removed from the so-called normality of daily life. These miners do not often see the light of day, but spend it in a kind of regular exile. Sometimes they do not return.

A friend has written from Australia, and comments on Yiayia's death. She remarks wisely (Amy's letters, which I have been receiving for sixteen years, are invariably wise) that the death seems strange; it is a disappearance of an apparently immovable presence. 'You both had passion . . . and you have ensured her immortality by writing about her.'

I am getting ready for a trip to Dublin, where I am to present a paper and read in august company. The butterflies in my stomach are very speedily attaining the dimensions of pterodactyls. But I get myself to Terminal One, Heathrow, where I have never been before. I prowl through glass and steel circles linked by corridors, sink into an appropriately green seat and watch a satellite disk whirling round. I look hopefully about me for anybody resembling an academic.

And then I spot one. He's chewing gum, a thing the academics of my youth would never have dreamed of, but they would never have dreamed of giving up smoking, either. He must be nervous because he's reading his paper over, and if I squint I can see the name of the conference written on it. I make sure my Akubra hat is very much in evidence but it does me no good. Soon I am in the plane and viewing pink-tinted, cotton-wool castles of cloud and the ordered, bordered patches of England.

It is a peculiar experience meeting the academics of one's youth after a gap of thirty years, and this happens several times because the conference is about Australian identity, whatever that means, which is, I suppose, the purpose of the conference: to hazard a guess. These figures from my past are now worthy pillars of academe, freed from the anxiety of having to publish, but not free, I gather, from worry about their superannuation and the state of their pockets. Close call, someone says, I nearly didn't get funding.

It is pointless to envy academics, whose lives are just as riven by pain and loss as anybody else's, and who are more tormented by envy and threatened ego and esteem than many. Envy doesn't do, it really doesn't, I tell myself sternly, while trying not to think about professorial salaries. Funding, indeed. What I will always envy, though, I suspect, is the quality I conspicuously lack: practical ruthlessness.

The days pass in a blur of stimulation: papers, poetry readings, discussions, arguments, and the game of oneupmanship, for which I have little talent even though I know the rules. What to *do* with all this input? Use it somehow, all being grist to the mill, particularly the bits about wandering, displaced people, returning migrants who cannot get over the feeling of being in two places at once. The academic first sighted at Heathrow waxes eloquent on the subject of the distant child; he and I fit into this category. The child has slipped beyond parental control in the most obvious way, but the parent can control the image he has of the child, he maintains. Why didn't I think of this before, when it seems so obvious? Children who have an active and continuing presence in their parents' lives suffer from the pressures and tensions of reality: I know my siblings have.

And then there are the stories about Greece, where a lively couple went to live in the '60s and '70s, long before I did, stories of playing guitars in brothels, of desperate passion and stabbings because of jealousy, of trickery and adventure. Descriptions of people and places untouched by tourism. I envy these people their experiences and memories. Their Greece was never mine, and now both are gone forever.

My preparation, because I am always passing through, is never enough. Little things, however, tend to stick to my fly-paper mind. 'I do think a *jackdaw* mind is so much more upmarket,' an Englishman corrected me once. 'I'm Australian,' I said, 'and therefore more used to flies.'

What I remember from my scant reading is merely shallow layers. The various populations in Ireland – the native Irish, then the Danish, Norwegians, Normans, Anglo-Normans, English and French – were attracted, as people always are, by a river, by its mouth and ford. The first reference to the town that became Dublin is to be found in the Greek geography of Claudius Ptolemy in 140 AD.

My guidebook is sentimental on the subject of the peat-coloured waters of the Liffey, but a river is a river, etc. At least in my opinion. The Danube was distinctly not blue on the one occasion I viewed it long ago, a circumstance which worried me at the time. Perhaps I could, at a pinch, yearn sentimentally for the muddy waters of the Yarra Yarra.

Dublin has had many famous visitors, including Odin the war god, who rode around on an apple-green charger on the eve of the Battle of Clontarf in 1014. Fast forward to Oliver Cromwell, who had a few churches desecrated in 1649. Charles II was declared king in Dublin before the Restoration, and James II passed through on the way to and from that conflict of far-reaching consequences and bitter memories, the Battle of the Boyne, in July 1690. William III also paid a visit.

For my part, all I can remember about Dublin is that one of my great-grandmothers, one Eliza, was married in St Mary's church here. Oh, but of course I remember sweet Mollie Malone, whose statue I glimpse from a bus window. No wonder she died of a fever, says my companion. Look at that bare chest.

There is not enough time, as usual, and I feel myself torn between the forms of learning on offer: conference papers and this beautiful, graceful city with its strata of troubled history. An inspection of the General Post Office, headquarters of the Irish Volunteers in 1916, is mandatory. The bullet pocks are pointed out to me and I remember others: the one in the wall of a church in Nafplion where Capodistrias, first president of the very new Greek republic, was assassinated one Sunday morning; others in the wall of the Hampstead pub outside which Ruth Ellis gunned down her unfaithful lover and then became the last woman to be hanged in Britain. Politics, passion and the passing of time. I know these episodes occurred, for the evidence tells me so, but I can't quite believe in them.

And the literature, the drama, the books and the writing. To the library at Trinity College where I wander around in a state of awed numbness, or numb awe. The beauty of it, the thought of its three million volumes, the idea of there having been a library on this site for more than four centuries. How can people talk of the post-literate age and the death of the book? It still needs half a mile of extra shelving a year. *Half a mile.*

At the Writers' Centre I buy a copy of *Ulysses.* A sure-fire cure for insomnia, says an irreverent Canadian companion.

Back in London Elizabeth tells me that Marlon Brando was in her Eurostar carriage on the way over from Paris. I'm glad I wasn't there, I decide. I want to remember him as he was in *Julius Caesar,* as he was in *On the Waterfront,* looking in the mirror and saying, 'I coulda bin a contender.'

Fighting Dr Johnson's black dog again. The slide into melancholy comes often as a result of the grey weather, but more often as a result of wounded ego: suffice it to say that I am tired of people who, refusing to practise the art of getting to know, write their brief letters on chunks of glacier instead of paper. (And the Royal Mail service is so good that the ice doesn't even have a chance to melt in transit.) I infer that their choice of stationery matches the slow-moving nature and content of their veins. They do not have arteries, these people who mercilessly coquette with friendship and cause an almost intolerable ache of the heart, for arterial blood is red and vital to life.

When the melancholy fit falls, it seems to me that my days pass swifter than a weaver's shuttle and are spent without hope, as Job, that old death's head at the feast, once said. Or words to that effect. Job at least had some excuse (boils are awful), but I have no right to be maundering on like this (unless of course self-indulgence and a good old wallow are among the inalienable rights of a person) after a day spent in that most elegant of places, Bath.

Ah, the creamed-honey city in the sunlight. All those curves, careful organisation and grace; all the symmetry of the terraced structures to the front and all the idiosyncrasy behind, the back of every building being different. Such designs are the perfect metaphor for the English temperament and character. Even the colour of the stone and the soft light and wisps of cloud assist the unity of this impression: let us, above all, be temperate. Civilisation, as we know and practise it, has nothing to do with passion (even the backs of our houses cannot be said to be unruly) and everything to do with good manners, courtesy, refinement and tranquillity. Starch, as Beau Brummel said, is everything. Let us appear, always, to be unruffled, certain of our dignity and place. Those who are uncertain of these things should not attempt, even if their need is great, or especially if their need is great, to knock at any of our doors, front or back.

The long, long chain of English history: Elizabeth lived in Bath in her youth and takes me to look at the Pump Room, where, she says, laughing, balls were held in Jane Austen's time and in hers. But Austen, despite using Bath as the setting for *Northanger Abbey* and *Persuasion*, and having her heroines find love here, found it a mite dull, and confessed to disordering her stomach with Bath 'bunns'. In the abbey Governor Phillip is remembered: an Australian flag droops above his memorial tablet. One could spend a week looking at the hundreds of tablets and gazing at the exquisite fan-vaulted ceiling.

The guidebook tells me that Bishop Oliver King was instructed in a dream to restore the church, which work he began in 1499. The bishop's dream, like Jacob's in the Old Testament, featured angels ascending and descending a ladder to Heaven. And here are two ladders, soaring on this particular day into a blue sky and being climbed, one knows instinctively, even though they are so distant, by perfectly formed little figures with sprouting wings and ordered draperies. One of the angels is upsidedown, the stonemason's way of depicting the descent. Faith and perfectionism. (In Exeter Cathedral the roof bosses are tiny figures of knights, perfectly sculpted, sitting sixty feet above the ground. Nobody except the original craftsmen and a church restorer has ever sighted them, yet they are perfectly formed because their makers were convinced that God could see them.)

In the gardens of Bath's Royal Crescent Hotel Elizabeth and I consume smoked-salmon sandwiches which ought to be platinum-plated, they cost so much. Correct young flunkeys float up and down the garden paths, past banks of lavender, masses of camomile and towers of roses, carrying one item at a time to various rooms: a glass of orange juice, a fluffy toy rabbit, an electric fan. A pair of shoe addicts a table away compare purchases while waiting for their second glasses of gin and tonic.

Beautiful, beautiful Bath, I sigh to myself as we leave, and then tell myself sternly that this promiscuity with regard to places has got to stop. So then I start sighing for Greece and for Jo as well, and feel, as I do so often, that I am swimming out of my depth with no hope of reaching any shore.

I have never been in England at this time of year before. The sun continues its pale shine; gardens bloom sweetly pretty. Ah, the softness and the courtesy and friendliness of the people: England as a cuddly blanket, an old familiar dressing-gown. Ugh! I hear a chorus of dissenters complaining, but I do not care. Let them migrate to a Peloponnesian village and then note the contrast: the Peloponnese is distinctly *not* cuddly!

Elizabeth is unhappy about the blue skies. 'England will soon be like the Sahara,' she considers, making the statement with a kind of gloomy satisfaction.

'Surely not,' I say to her. 'Not in our lifetime. *Après nous le désert*, and all that.'

'There'll always be an England, even if only in Hollywood,' said Bob Hope.

Why am I always meeting slightly dotty men? Mrs Bourke claims she does, too. 'Crrrackers, t'ey are!'

'Watch out,' I grin. 'There's somebody out there waiting to sweep you off your feet and take you away from all this.'

'What rubbish you talk,' she remarks.

This morning's episode: in the supermarket check-out queue I found myself behind a bald-pated chap of uncertain age and exact Oxford accent, and presented him with a banana which he'd accidentally left behind.

'Thank you *so* much,' he trilled. Predictably. And then wanted to know whether I'd ever walked from Haverstock Hill to Oxford Street.

'Er no,' I replied. 'How long does it take?'

'Through Primrose Hill and Regent's Park, an hour.'

'Oh. Well, I *have* walked from Trafalgar Square to just past the Broad Walk in Kensington Gardens.' It took me two hours, but I dawdled and dropped in at St James's, Piccadilly, on the way. 'Do you do this for pleasure, not in any spirit of competition?' I asked.

'Competition? Against whom?'

'Oh, I don't know. Against yourself? Bettering your time, perhaps?'

'Ludicrous, the mere idea,' he declared roundly. (The world is made up of two types of people: those who know they are right, and those who worry that they almost never are, and I know which category I fall into. Repeatedly. Here I *do* fit.) Then he relented slightly, eyed me solemnly and intoned, 'We are going nowhere; we are already here.'

'Interesting thought,' I rallied, annoyed with myself for not being able to place it: Camus? Beckett?

But it's not interesting. It's depressing, and an idea that awakens some of my deepest fears. I much prefer Dickens: 'The journey is ever onward, after all.'

To the British Museum in order to attend a lecture on icons, an excursion which would seem to have the character of a backward journey if ever there was one, but never mind. I learn (as if I needed to) that there is a close connection between women and the veneration of icons. Other snippets of information stick, in the usual way: St Peter always has white hair and a well-cut white beard. I think he nearly always holds the keys of Heaven as well. In Ravenna the twelve apostles are depicted as sheep. Now that is something I didn't know. The Byzantine belief was that St Luke painted the Holy Family from life. Aghia Sophia is itself an iconic image. The audience, for the most part, is very interested, very earnest and very old. One man is literally asleep on his feet, a curious sight. But perhaps he is merely resting his eyes.

It is only a short walk across to the old British Library, to an exhibition on the subject of quests. Naturally I feel compelled to go. Quests, historically speaking, seem to aim for everlasting love, heroic glory, spiritual enlightenment. When it comes to my own historical narrative, I decide to give the second a miss: mustn't be greedy.

The exhibition tells marvellous stories; not unnaturally, it is the section on Alexander the Great that demands my interest and my time. The First Book of Maccabees states matter-of-factly that Alexander 'undertook many campaigns, gained possession of many fortresses, and put the local kings to death. He advanced to the ends of the earth, plundering nation after nation; the earth grew silent before him . . .' But the exhibition writer considers that he was an anticipation of Christ, in that he pressed against the boundaries of the known world. He even went diving in a kind of submarine bell arrangement, taking a cat, a cock and a dog with him. The cat was to keep the air circulating by taking in Alexander's breath and then returning it: the old idea of cats sucking babies' breath seems to make sense, after all. The cock was to act as a kind of calendar, marking out the days by its crowing, and the dog was a means of escape: if danger threatened, the dog would be killed and the others saved, as the sea would not tolerate pollution by blood, and would cast Alexander and company up on the nearest available shore. Alexander, I have read, was very keen on the notion of eternal life, but his sister accidentally spilled the glass of the water which guaranteed this, so he had her turned into an immortal and particularly restless sort of mermaid who has the ability to cause tumultuous storms at sea.

I visit the Silver Vaults with Max, who is toting a Georgian teapot dated 1824 and wants to organise the repair of its handle. Dazzle, dazzle, gasp, gasp, and I decide that my life is empty without a claret jug. Of course there are about four hundred reasons why I will never have said item, most of them to do with pounds, but still. Some of the things — utensils, pieces of equipment — simply baffle me. What are they *for?* Kitsch is here in expensive abundance: statuettes constructed out of silver and blown glass with coloured swirly patterns, deeply vulgar rings, items which are quite simply gewgaws. (How nicely vulgar that word sounds: on a par with 'tawdry trinkets' and 'trumpery'.)

In flibbertigibbet mode, I do not want the afternoon to end, so Max kindly takes me to St Etheldreda's in Ely Place, a church that was restored to the 'old faith' last century. St Etheldreda, I'm told, was some sort of professional virgin who married X number of men but kept proclaiming that her One True Love was God, and that, as a consequence, she could Know No Other, or words to that effect. Whether her husbands died of extreme frustration is not recorded. The walls of the church are home to statues of many martyrs who came

168

to various grisly ends, mainly as a punishment for har-
bouring priests.

Back at home a phone call informs me of the fact
that a female guest has been struck by lightning at the
Queen's garden party. Obviously the republican
movement invoking higher powers.

AUGUST

Quests. Pilgrimages. And so to Haworth, where I have longed to go for thirty-five years. We set off, Kay and I, the car purring through the leafy tunnels of Lancashire and Yorkshire. The sheep, often to be seen wandering along lanes and roads, vary with the landscape and some wear coats of ground-length straight wool, a strange sight for one so accustomed to the appearance of merinos. Kay tells me that the Dutch are about to allow sheep on their roads in direct imitation of Yorkshire habits – as a measure against speeding.

The landscape is divided into impossibly green squares and rectangles, with great sweeps of brown moor edged by dry walls which have kinks in them, unlike the Australian ones I remember, which stretch away in slightly bumpy straight lines for miles. Clouds tower in a washed sky.

Haworth is tourist-pretty on a fine day, but I learn that Charlotte Brontë, when inviting Mrs Gaskell to stay, wrote of the comparison between it and the back-woods of America. 'You must come out to barbarism, loneliness and liberty.' It seems to have been a shock-ingly unhealthy place, where people died like flies because of a polluted water supply: Haworth was an industrial area. The parsonage appears refined and romantic in this fickle summer, but must be wretchedly cold at other times of the year.

It is difficult to write about the homes of the famous. I quite simply do not know what to say about the walls and roofs that sheltered these imperishable spirits. It is, of course, a pleasure to match environment and writ-ing, to see pieces of furniture that rate a mention in the books, to apprehend even dimly the short crammed lives of the sisters, the waste of Branwell's life, and the irony of the fact that Patrick Brontë, their father, who does not sound My Type at all, outlived every one of his children. That seems to me to be one of the saddest fates a person can have. And then there is the contrast between refinement, with its rules for living, and the passions, the latter of which at least rehearsed the idea of breaking those rules.

It is the voices which are important, which call down the long, long tunnel of years and still seem familiar: there is no hint of distance. Charlotte on teaching: 'I sat sinking from irritation and weariness into a kind of lethargy.' How every teacher understands. I wouldn't mind betting she wrote that particular fragment of deathless prose on a Friday afternoon. Even Robert Southey is a type I recognise as one who would do very well in the Peloponnese of the 1990s. 'Literature,' he informed the 21-year-old Charlotte, 'cannot be the business of a woman's life, and it ought not to be. The more she is engaged in her proper duties, the less leisure she will have for it, even as an accomplishment.' Hmm. How familiar that sounds, indeed. All that is needed is a Greek translation. Modern Greek. I don't think it was Southey's instinctive guess that literature breeds distress; he was merely a Victorian chauvinist.

Charlotte's husband, the Reverend Nicholls, worried about her letter-writing. He seems to have been a very private person who fretted about the possibility of her letters falling into the wrong hands or being used in the wrong way. Charlotte asked her friend Ellen Nussey to destroy her letters, but Ellen was sensibly disobedient. The reverend gentleman, it appears, considered women in general 'most rash in letter-writing' and Charlotte's letters in particular 'as dangerous as lucifer candles'. I read this and laughed, having lit a few lucifer candles in my time; at least I've always been prepared to have my fingers burnt, or even my eyebrows singed.

Back in London, and Mick rings to tell me how great it is to abseil from a helicopter. 'Oh yes,' I say, practising British phlegm like mad but inwardly feeling sick. 'So good of you to ring *after* rather than before.'

'Yeah,' he agrees, 'especially seeing that the bloke who went before me shot straight down onto the tarmac and broke a leg.'

Later, while Mick is enduring five nights' compulsory sleep deprivation and other horrors while being tested on all he has learned during a frogmen's training course, my telephone comes to resemble a rattlesnake

waiting to strike. On the Saturday it rings with good
news: he has passed and survived. I have bargained with
God again, and so I go to church on Sunday.

Reading about Greece. Peter Levi, that great philhellene, describes Kalamata as a strange corner of
the provinces, a description with which I agree.
A travel journalist makes the very sound observation
that the Greeks might have led the world culturally
but they never won any prizes for plumbing. He also
advises sagely on the necessity for a sense of humour
when visiting Greece. He's not wrong.

But perhaps it is true to say that Greece stimulates
a sense of humour in ways not thought of before. The
sheer authenticity and vitality of Greek behaviour, and
the streak of anarchy which seems built into every
Greek soul, can be immensely attractive, and even the
raised noise levels suggest a kind of tuning in to cosmic
energies; in a sense Greeks, in their impulsiveness and
spontaneity, enact what in other cultures remain fan-
tasies. Kavafis put it very well when he said that Greeks
approach life and the universe at a slight angle. I once

saw an elderly woman emerge from the Kalamata post office, face wreathed in smiles, holding a large parcel and making her way down the several steps very carefully. As soon as she was safely on the pavement she kissed the parcel not just once but several times. At Athens airport recently I saw a chortling English tourist take a picture of a notice in Greek and English: 'Passengers are requested not to leave luggage unattended in the terminal area.' Neatly piled under the notice were three large bags and four overcoats.

I was in an Athens bus when the driver, impatient with the snarl of traffic near the Temple of Olympian Zeus, calmly drove up and over the median strip, parked the bus on the wrong side of the road and told the passengers to walk into town. On an island some time ago, passengers in a bus took a vote and decided they didn't want to go to the destination advertised on the front of the bus; the only two people wanting to go there were Australian tourists, who were politely offloaded and told that a taxi would come along the road sooner or later. It did, fortunately sooner.

Such impulsiveness has its shadow side, however. It is difficult to know what complexities lead to the act of suicide, but I wonder whether complexities actually exist in the case of Greek suicides, which often seem to occur on the spur of the moment, but are generally successful rather than mere attempts and cries for help. People hang themselves and throw themselves down wells. One spring there were three suicides by hanging in the immediate vicinity of the village. The tendency is to act rather than think, and passion rather than introspection rules. No wonder that Greeks, when in conflict with the products of Western culture with its emphasis on restraint and reason, feel that there is nothing very much to engage with, that the gladiators have no one to contend with. Very frustrating, they must find it.

I myself am engaged in a kind of pendulum swing, as perhaps many white Australians are. We have the authenticity of a scarcely known continent as background or roots, yet yearn for the layers of what the world is pleased to call culture and civilisation. Tradition fits in there somewhere, too, and presents a problem for Australians of my generation, European in outlook but now having to look towards Asia; the current generation is engaged in the richly creative process of fusing, of putting down a new layer on the palimpsest which is Australia.

One reason Cornwall demands my attention is because it is on the edge of the world, like the Peloponnese, like Cardiff, like the south-west coast of Victoria, Australia. It, like Melbourne, keeps drawing me back, although the weather in winter and spring is so uniformly atrocious that I do not wonder that my ancestors, having extricated themselves from dark, satanic tin mines, fled to sunny South Australia. Clearly they had get-up-and-go; they got up and went. Then, perhaps missing what a Cornish friend calls the drama of weather, they relocated to Victoria. In the case of the great-great-grandmother who lost her husband to 'colonial fever' after six weeks in the colony, the relocation was by no means easy: legend has it that she and her two children took another six weeks, travelling by bullock dray, to reach contacts on the Victorian gold fields. Her few banknotes were, in time-honoured fashion, stuffed in her garter.

These edge-of-the-world places pride themselves on

their difference. In Cornwall the black and white flag flies; separatist racist graffiti amuses me, detached outsider that I am: 'Be a good Cornishman: kill a Spanish bastard.' Perhaps I should not be so amused; my livelihood is threatened by publishers, agents, and readers, not by the Spanish fishing fleet. This killing business has been going on for an awfully long time, though: Squire Keigwin of Mousehole, for example, died in 1595 while defending his home against Spanish raiders, who clearly hadn't learned a thing from the example of the Armada.

And of course Cornwall appeals: ancestral voices call and mix with memories of childhood, for my earliest holidays were spent on the Victorian coast, with the weight of the vast continent pressing behind and the limitless ocean beckoning ahead, where Antarctica and the bottom of the world lay. The Cornish coast is like it and like the Peloponnesian one, and recalls Kitries, Akroyiali, Oitilo, Kardamili, and the music of the place names I once thought so strange. There are caves and cracks and scree and long rollers the swirling aqua-navy colour of the Southern Ocean. And it appeals for its own sake.

The first long walk I ever did, from Porthcurno to

Land's End, was full of the aforementioned drama of weather, taking place in a howling gale and culminating in a hailstorm. Flakes of foam flew through the air like snow, and in a rare sunny break a pair of courting crows performed a ballet in mid-air, swooping, curving, meeting and diving against a sky that was very briefly blue. It was all supremely worth it, despite my fear of being blown over a cliff and even though I poured quantities of water out of my boots at Land's End and was forced to wring my socks out as well.

Amy went to Cornwall once and a notice in her hotel read, 'It's not whether you like Cornwall, it's whether Cornwall likes you.' Perhaps the relationship between Cornwall and me is a genuine one, for it is certainly marked by ambivalence on my part. I do not want to stay there, but every time I leave I am reminded of the true nature of my heart, that vast echo chamber of farewells.

And in Cornwall I am haunted by unexpected ghosts, for in Zennor Church is the famous mermaid chair. The mermaid is the symbol of Aphrodite, goddess of sea and love – who would have thought that my redoubtable Greek mother-in-law would hold sway even here? Once upon a time this smooth dark carving used to hold a quince, a love apple, in one hand, and a comb in the other, but the quince was later changed to a mirror, symbol of vanity and heartlessness. And suddenly I see my Aphrodite as she had been so often in the past, seated by her window, combing her long greying tresses in a steady rhythm. Although I have written about her and have mentioned mirrors, I never considered her heartless. Vain, yes; she had quite a lot to be vain about. Her heart, however, was insulated – it had had to be in order for her to survive – and in her old age, it seemed to me, she saw no point in unwrapping the protective layers, particularly for the sake of a stubborn, impractical stranger.

I learn, standing in Zennor Church, that during the Middle Ages, when the Cornish mystery plays were performed, the mermaid was used to represent the nature of Christ: she was both human and fish, he was God and man. Aphrodite – my mother-in-law, not the goddess – was clearly in a unique category. No wonder she made me feel weak in response to her power, reduced by it in her presence.

There are three of us wandering round Zennor and

a local remarks to us while we are in the churchyard, 'You're not from here, are you? Any of you?'

These are actually statements rather than questions but, 'How long does it take?' asks one of my companions. 'I've lived here for forty years.'

'Three hundred,' is the reply. I say nothing, but I am the one who qualifies in a way, as my ancestors were certainly grubbing around in the dirt not far from here three hundred years ago. I also look the part, being short, stumpy-legged and dark.

It is in Cornwall that I discover, quite accidentally, a poem called 'Lasca' by someone called Duprez. A line from this poem has haunted me forever because my grandmother used to recite dramatically, 'Down came the mustang and down came we, clinging together . . .' But my memory has consistently failed to yield up any more, and now suddenly here is a verse at least, and I realise that my very young memory retained the one line it was capable of understanding, the line that tells of life and drama.

I gouged out a grave a few feet deep
And there in earth's arms I laid her to sleep

And I wonder why I do not care
For things that are, like the things that were:
Does half my heart lie buried there,
In Texas, down by the Rio Grande?

I understand now, and know why I do not care for
things that are, or not for very many of them, but cannot decide whether any part of my heart, that
unreliable and now redundant organ, is actually buried
anywhere, or whether, rather, I have left bits and
pieces of my essential self in such varied places that my
heart and I are in a state of at least partial disintegration. And then there's the nasty thought, not an
original one but very accurate, that we tend, despite
everything, to be attached to our predicaments.
Perhaps the process of slow disintegration, both
psychical and physical, suits me.

My heart can also be considered an echo chamber
of farewells; despite this it still remains optimistically
ready to say G'day to kindred spirits, and so today I am
consoled by the very easy company of an Australian
man of about my own age. He is travelling from Truro
to Plymouth in order to see friends of friends and to

deliver a packet of photographs from New South Wales. (Ah, the ways of the Antipodean traveller.) When he gets into the train I am reading a Thomas Keneally novel, reading about Sydney beaches while tearing through the green and wooded Cornish countryside. Close by, a teenage girl is reading a book called *Dreams that Came True*. Why is she wasting her time? I ask myself, but remind myself that, yes, indeed, I was a teenager once, right after they had just been invented.

The traveller is from South Australia, which is almost another foreign land, even though I have been to Adelaide, but still, I feel a dreadful pang of homesickness when he leaves the train. He is from the country, but is by no means unsophisticated and retains a lively curiosity, so much a part, I have learned, of New World intelligence. We talk about trees, and did I know that German contains a word for forest-murder? We talk about snakes: 'The old death adder is pretty good, ya have to tease it quite a bit before it goes for ya.' We talk about rivers and boats and horse-racing and our ancestors and the deaths of our mothers, the way of governments and their insatiable thirst for taxes, and about corporate baddies and hitchhikers and murderers. Oh, and *Zorba the Greek*.

'Ya gotta keep on the move,' he maintains. 'Check the environment, be aware of ecology, keep walking. Walking unstresses ya. Ya can't afford to go backwards. Tess of the d'Urbervilles did and look what happened to her.' This remark unsettles me, as I fear that I have been going backwards for some considerable time, or rather, I cannot decide in which direction I am headed. I also fear that the President of the Immortals has not finished his sport with me yet. (At the risk of sounding just a mite egotistical.)

I rally, though, and mention Richard Mahony.

'Crikey, that bloke. Yeah, well, see? You've lost yer accent, by the way.'

'That's what Australians always think,' I tell him, and do not mention that I am twitted about my accent wherever I go.

A minute before leaving he is still talking earnestly about silt in the Tamar and how he wouldn't come to England again, ''cos Australia's more beautiful, I reckon. London's worth a day, d' ya reckon?'

'Yes,' I state very firmly, 'yes. Bye.'

'See yez,' he says, knowing full well he won't.

Another item for the fly-paper mind: in the tenth century the Grand Vizier of Persia owned 117 000 books and could not bear to be parted from them, and so he also owned four hundred camels which were trained to walk in alphabetical order. I wonder what Dewey would have thought of *that*.

It is my birthday and I am delighted to be taken to a village cricket match in Hertfordshire. The day is *hot* and I cannot quite believe this, despite the usual sensations, never having been hot in England before. A weak warm is about all I have managed to feel until now. My hosts and I sit under a wide blue sky with its miraculous lack of cloud and feel as if we are part of the cricketing scene in that memorable film *The Go-Between*. Hampers and deck-chairs and dogs and whites that could be whiter and warm drinks and young Australian men who show the rest, quite rightly, a thing or two about this noble game. My sons, of course, consider it quite pointless. I can't blame Jo for this attitude, but the others, having been born in Australia, ought to know better. And cricket is still played on the island of Corfu, after all.

To the Reform Club. Another accident, because I know someone who knows someone who is about to launch a book about cricket on Sir Donald Bradman's birthday. The Reform Club is overwhelming in every way, but at least I can talk about having attended matches on Corfu and at the MCG. The great and the good of the cricket world are here. 'Who's that pleasant chap I've just been talking to?' I hiss to my friend.

'Oh, for God's sake, don't you know anything or anybody?' And a very famous cricket knight is named. Sir Colin Cowdrey. His parents were so fanatical about cricket, I'm told, they made sure his initials spelt MCC.

'Oh,' I say. I'm always saying Oh. My father will be thrilled.

Then I am introduced to an ancient lord who refuses to sit while a lady is standing. Not knowing quite what to say, let alone how to address him, I murmur my thanks and look about rather desperately for chairs. He looks hale enough, but I worry about him and really consider that the forty years' difference in our ages is sufficient excuse for the immediate relaxation of these ramrod standards. But how can I say this? The woman near me produces her glasses and it turns out that his lordship has a pronounced spectacles fetish. Well, I suppose any sort of fetish is okay when you'll never see ninety again: age must have some benefits and privileges. 'D' you wear glasses, m'dear?' he enquires.

'Yes,' I reply, 'but I've left them at home.'

'Great pity,' he announces, and gazes into space. Well, at least he's not like my Greek sisters-in-law and going on about my grey hair. I introduce the topic of his writer daughter, whose work I greatly admire.

'*Poor* T,' he mourns. 'She works *so* hard.' I grit my teeth and forbear to mention the hard work of the reviewers who are unanimous in their praise, and of course it would be just too vulgar and crass to mention the hard work put in by booksellers, readers, cashiers and accountants. Jealousy is a frightfully ugly thing.

On the platform at Charing Cross a man is sitting reading *The Cretan Runner*. I resist the temptation to yell, 'Hey, I know people who know old George Psychoundakis; and the great Patrick Leigh Fermor, Michali in the book and in his wartime Cretan life, lives not far away from where I live in the Peloponnese. Small world and all that.' But of course I'm not a name-dropper. Heaven forbid. Which reminds me of the anecdote I have dined out on many times. One of Her Majesty's very eminent clerics, now dead, had the reputation of being an outrageous snob and was heard to remark, 'I hate name-droppers, and so does the Queen.'

The rest of the month passes in a haze: work, Australian visitors and theatre excursions. At a production of *The Phoenician Women* a member of the theatre staff hands out sprigs of basil. Very aromatic, very Greek, he announces in a patronising tone. Yes. Indeed. On a Greek mountainside, but not in the carpeted, dim atmosphere of The Pit. The production is powerful, though, with lots of the requisite terror and pity.

Nothing much has changed, clearly, in two thousand years or so, but it's a peculiar feeling seeing Greek theatre on this minute scale.

My fifth visit to Scotland, to yet another conference: how strange it seems now to think that I once despaired of ever visiting this place, yet another ancestral haunt of love and memory. In the carriage is an older Scottish woman (sensible hair, serviceable coat, case in a subdued tartan, travelling rug) who has been in Sussex for a month and cannot wait to get back to Edinburgh. She spends most of the journey absorbed in a battered copy of John Buchan's *Mr Standfast*, the existence of which volume I had completely forgotten. Next to me sits a bottle-blonde who is dripping with costume jewellery: her choice of literature is one of a series called something like 'Silhouettes of Desire', and the particular title which engrosses her for miles is *Beware: Men at Play*. As we cross the border she tells me how much she likes Sydney; she has stayed in Coogee. There is also a party of young Greek men, clearly students. Of course they use their favourite swear word constantly and I pretend that I do not understand what they are talking about. They are much noisier than the rest of us, but also very courteous and kind to older passengers, heaving luggage about and opening doors.

It seems to me that academic conferences are wonderful holidays. The only restriction on freedom is the necessity to present a paper – the rest is dedicated to fun, although it has to be said that papers are a pest and conducive to feelings of severe anxiety. A lecturer makes the point that men start their papers with jokes, women with apologies. I must remember that.

Once again this is an Australian conference, so it is not really surprising that the vast majority of people elect to go to see the ship called *City of Adelaide*, one of two options for the conference excursion. This ship, reputed to be one of the world's oldest clippers, is moored in the River Irvine at the Scottish Maritime Museum, and is a very sobering sight. Once a year she would go to Adelaide with cargo (including cricket bats) and passengers, and return mainly with cargo. It is claimed that one of her voyages took only sixty-five days, a record. She was built to carry two hundred and seventy passengers but her vital statistics boggle the modern mind. She is 176 feet long, 33 feet wide and 900 tons in weight. She looks the wreck she is, but the aim is complete restoration, for she is so well documented that social and economic historians are entranced.

So are the women of the party. Our minds immediately turn to the subjects of crinolines, petticoats, washing, periods, smells, layers of perfumes and powder, sanitation, constipation, the toilet-training of toddlers, for there surely must have been some. And how were they prevented from falling overboard? Then there is the question of mental health. Close company can save you from depression but can also drive you into it. I am quite sure that, hounded by the black dog and incompatible people, I would have jumped into the sea at the end of a week. There are two recorded cases of people doing this, which seems a very low score indeed to me. Attitudes were different, of course. My ancestors would have commended their bodies and souls to the care of Almighty God and simply set about the task of enduring the voyage.

I am lost in admiration of my ancestral genes and feel a surge of confidence in my own, and remark as much to somebody, but the resident expert is here to tell us that one's ancestral genes very nearly didn't make it, and proceeds to relate horrifying stories of typhoid epidemics and similar blights.

This conference will be hard to beat, we all agree, after drinks on a naturally formed terrace at Stirling Castle, after the ritual piping into the castle on a balmy evening. Past and present collide as I meet the man who has the dubious distinction of being my first ever English tutor. We agree it is a strange feeling to be meeting again after so long and in such different circumstances. Within an hour or two we are whirling and twirling at the *ceilidh*, after a mistress of ceremonies has given us 'a wee walk threw' of various steps, after which I discover that the Gay Gordons and two glasses of claret are a combination not to be recommended. I also consider that the Dashing White Sergeant will never be the same again.

There is a great deal of eating going on; in fact, the Scots could rival the Greeks. I am surrounded by Australian male academics who all seem to be good trencher-persons and hence critical of my tendency to leave food on my plate. 'What's that?' I ask suspiciously when a blood-coloured concoction marooned in a sea of cream appears in front of me. 'Raspberry haggis,' is the suggestion.

Scotland and Greece: the links are many, and indeed the word *scotia* means dark in Greek. The soil in both places is soaked in blood. (I have heard of an Australian who couldn't stay in Europe because she couldn't bear the idea of walking on top of so much blood.) Stirling, a kind of fortress-crowned rock with the grey town clinging to its sides, is the scene of seven major battles, and many a dark deed has been done in the place where we are dancing. In 1452 James II stabbed the eighth Earl of Douglas to death in what is now referred to as the Douglas Room, and threw his body out of the window at the end of the passage.

Formative influences were at least in part responsible for the violence of this particular act. When he was eight years old the boy-king had seen the sixth Earl of Douglas, who was only fourteen, and the Earl's younger brother murdered, more or less at the dinner table, in Edinburgh Castle. The two boys had been summoned to a banquet at which the head of a black bull was brought in. This was the sentence of death, very speedily carried out. Even though they were very young, the Douglases had become too powerful and were thus feared by those closest to the King. The nobles Crichton and Livingstone appear to have been involved in this judicial murder. The banquet became known as the black *dinoir* and the criminals were never punished.

I thought Northumberland was littered with castles – twenty-eight is the number – but Scotland probably rivals this. Castle Campbell is only twelve miles away, but it took Mary, Queen of Scots three days to get there in order to attend a wedding one January. One wonders about the prospects of conjugal bliss, about the dire nature of the Scottish winter, and about the fact that the castle was once known as The Gloume and is situated above the Burn of Care and the Burn of Sorrow. John Knox preached there, which seems appropriate, mirth never having been associated with that particular gentleman, and Montrose's army tried in 1645 to take it and failed. It would be a hard place to take, isolated on a spur as it is. Some of Montrose's troops, conducting a private feud with the Campbells, which seems to have been a popular pastime through the centuries, wanted to burn it.

General Monk arrived nine years later and made a better job of destruction. Cromwell's Monk seems to have been pretty good at destruction, but fortunately did not do too much damage at Rosslyn Chapel, near Edinburgh, despite the fact that he stabled both his horses and his troops within its richly carved walls. But this sandstone building was supposed to be a Masonic temple, and Monk doubtless remained on his best behaviour because he knew that Cromwell was a Grand Master Mason.

William St Clair, Prince of Orkney, who founded Rosslyn Chapel in 1446 as an act of atonement for an extravagant life, was in the habit of eating his dinners off gold plate; his wife, Elizabeth, went hunting with a mounted escort of two hundred. No Greta Garbo tendencies there. Life being fairly nasty, brutish and short in the fifteenth century, people probably craved company rather than solitude. You never knew when you might be bumped off, as in death, not as in riding.

Back in Stirling, both James III and James IV kept lions, and one wonders whether they, too, were murder weapons. At James V's wedding the fountains ran with claret. But in the eighteenth century, the

Hanoverians, not an environmentally conscious lot, ordered the constant felling of trees so that the Jacobites would have nowhere to hide.

The tendency of my mind to be like fly-paper is exacerbated by the world of academe: the fly-paper unrolls its length and I become flippant and frivolous. It's not hard.

SEPTEMBER

A bad attack of post-conference *tristesse*: missing the atmosphere, missing Australians, just plain missing. There is always something and somebody absent. Life seems to be a matter of coping with the changing shape of things. I'm in a train again and trying to remember who said that if you want to write you have to come from somewhere. But it was William Faulkner who said that the only thing worth writing about is the problem of the human heart in conflict with itself. Well, there's lots of conflict within this particular breast, and that is the main reason I keep on the move. It's a distraction device.

So now I am on my way out of Greece again, having checked the three boys before going to Konstanz,

Germany, via Zurich, in my incarnation for this year only as conference junkie. On my way back from the village to Athens the bus stops at an unfamiliar souvlaki joint, where clearly the builder had come across a bargain in the form of mirrors. They are everywhere, including both sides of the loo doors, so that one is treated to the unedifying spectacle of oneself enthroned – or not, in obedience to one's safety-conscious grandmothers.

A mini-drama ensues when two widows of uncertain age but certainly dyed hair, who are dripping with huge jewellery, their ankles bulging over black wedge sandals, nearly miss the bus, having got onto another one by mistake.

The taxi queue is awful. Forty minutes of queue jumping, yelling and disorder. How this place is ever going to cope with the logistical demands of the Olympic Games is beyond the imaginations of a great many people. The police come and are absolutely useless; nobody takes a blind bit of notice of them, anyway. If you ever want to see naked self-interest in operation at its most extreme, then join (and I use the word loosely) an Athenian taxi queue (again I use the word loosely). Other attractions include the pack of stray dogs that prowl the bus station. There is a constant turnover of these animals, but a gang of some sort is always here.

There is usually something idiosyncratic in Greek hotels. Tonight I notice that over the bathroom basin the taps have been reversed, so that cold water comes out of the red-marked tap and hot comes out of the one decorated with blue.

My trip through Switzerland resembled clockwork. A nervous traveller, I was sure that the eight minutes I had in which to change trains for Konstanz would not be sufficient, but all I had to do was stroll from one platform to another. In Switzerland trains just glide away. At Zurich airport trolleys go on escalators – unbelievable bliss.

Along the railway track groaning apple trees are propped up: this season of mists and mellow fruitfulness seems already well advanced. There are neat little allotments, all with identical potting-sheds and Swiss flags very much in evidence. Even the autumnal flowers, chrysanthemums and dahlias, manage their blazes of colour tidily; the Virginia creeper is on the turn, and there are hints and tints of red and yellow. Years ago a friend remarked that all of Switzerland is shampooed and hung out to dry every morning. Now it seems to me that it primps and prinks like an attractive but rather complacent matron.

At Konstanz station the taxi driver asks me about my Akubra hat, and I manage, with my non-existent German, to explain about Australia. He beams. 'Australia, ja? Kangaroo, hop, hop, hop?'

'Ja,' I nod vigorously.

I feel very foreign in Konstanz, and also very ignorant. It is a long time since I felt so helpless and deprived of language, my Greek being adequate and my travel routes conventional and predictable. In the afternoon I manage to buy an ice-cream and also manage to avoid death by bicycle, having observed the native practice of tearing along the pavement on said vehicle. It doesn't seem to matter how fast you go as long as you ring the bicycle bell loudly and continuously. It never occurs to these cyclists that there are deaf foreigners walking the streets.

I scratch around for the little information that is available to the anglophone. Constantia was first mentioned in the year 525, when a travel writer called Anarid the Ostrogoth referred to it in a mini-guide. Now, there's a name for a writer, and one that would look good on any bestseller list, ancient or modern. Much later the town was the stage for the drama of the Great Schism of the Western Church, which began in 1378, was enacted for over forty years from 1378–1429, and for a little while it was the centre of Western Christendom, so that between 1414 and 1418 the emperor Sigismund and various princes of the Church, with hangers-on like abbots and bishops, lived here in a great wave of ecclesiastical immigration. In 1417 Martin V was elected and recognised as the only pope, and that stopped the schismatic rot, at least for the time being.

Of more relevance to me and my ancestors is the fact that John Hus, called by my guidebook a precursor of Protestantism and a hero of the Czech nation, was burned to death here on July the 6th, 1415. Any sort of martyrdom is sickening to contemplate: it is to be hoped that he died of smoke inhalation very quickly. He was everything the ancestors approved of: anti-confession, anti-Eucharist, anti-apostolic primacy. His ashes were scattered on the Rhine; his disciples struggled on.

The conference topic is 'New Literatures in English', and in between sessions I scoot round the place, suffering from a surfeit of impressions: painted buildings with their unfamiliar scalloped shapes decorated with extravagant coats of arms, Gothic spires, bronze statues, the huge scale of Lake Konstanz, the island of Mainau with its stylised waterfall and hanging garden and its huge topiary of birds and animals (I photographed the owl for Jo), and the thought of all those borders. ('I walked to Switzerland today,' announces a professor importantly. 'Gosh,' I say, impressed. 'How far is that?' 'About four blocks,' he replies.) The geography and history defeat me, and I wish I were much more like Patrick Leigh Fermor, who not only writes like an angel but has done a lot of homework.

I make the acquaintance of a group of New Zealanders who regale me with details of a German textbook about Australia. 'The native animals of Australia include various marsupials such as the kangaroo, the koala and the wattle.' We decide that if we see a wattle in the street we had better shoot it.

And before I know it I am on my way back to the village again, back the way I came, with the train shrieking and whistling through great cathedrals of forest, ghostly in the morning mist. The pines are still soaring and the apple trees are still propped up and weighed down. At Zurich airport I suffer from a sort of currency fatigue, for I have Swiss francs, deutschmarks, drachmae and sterling, and their various exchange rates floating around in my head. Still, I manage to buy a Swiss army knife for Jo.

And then I am flying over the Swiss Alps. At least I presume I am. Sometimes I long to be a geologist, having given up hope of ever being a geographer; at other times I'm glad I'm nothing in particular, as I do not want or need an explanation of a miracle, of the frosted jags and peaks looking like some impossibly huge confection of whipped cream and meringue.

Train/plane/taxi/bus/car, and then it is back to the important things in life: Jo turns his Greek-green eyes upon me sorrowfully because G has ordered him to have his hair cut and there is nothing he can do about this. Except obey. Unwillingly. Tom has finished his national service and found a flat in Athens, and Mick is about to start parachute training and I do not want to think about it. And elections are about to happen.

I am tired and feeling very self-indulgent and the world is in a mess and I wonder whether God regrets the particular direction His creativity has taken, post-Noah and the Ark, and thinks that it might have been a better idea to take up Fair Isle knitting or embroidery instead.

Today, curiosity combined with a lingering sense of duty leads me to go to inspect Aphrodite's – my mother-in-law's – grave. When I left at the end of June, wearing deep black in 40°C heat, I said goodbye to a mound of earth which boasted a makeshift cross, a big brown Nescafé jar crammed with flowers, and half a rusted kerosene tin which was sheltering the necessary candles.

I wander along to the graveyard after the manda-tory visit to the post office. I wear my sunglasses and hold my head high, but do not look at anybody. I do not want to be approached; I dread questions. Nothing changes much. The same men are sitting outside the *kafeneion*, the school is still flying the flag, but of course a new generation of children is playing in the yard. It does not seem very long since I took Tom and Mick there on their first day, the day of the education transplantation from Australia, but it is nearly sixteen years since that day we were all so nervous. I think I was probably more nervous than they, but at least I did not have the ordeal of sitting in the classroom.

I avoid the front entrance to the church and enter the graveyard via the back way. Aphrodite's grave is grey marble and topped with marble chips and a cross. There are lamps and a vase at the four corners. As is the custom, the grave has a little glass cupboard and shelf arrangement. Incised into this are the letters Alpha and Omega and a couple of stars. On the shelf rests a photo of Yiayia. I see her intimidating gaze again, or would the word implacable be better? There is also a piece of her own crochet, a little runner in white. It is, like all her work, exquisite. I stand in the churchyard where I have stood countless times before. Greece, the village, death. I have reached the age and stage at which I can expect to be notified of death on a fairly regular basis, and yesterday I received news of yet another death in Australia. There is a slight heat-mist on the mountains; near the charnel-house the oleanders are in bloom. Purple and red bougainvilleas are in bright blaze and somebody has put a sprig of the purple one on Yiayia's grave. There is also a red rose, fading now: its petals are overblown and starting to fall. I have not thought to bring flowers.

I stare myopically at what appears to be a fat, twisted, pale worm, but then realise it is a candle that has been dropped and has begun to melt.

Two workers on the church roof sit on the ridge-pole and chatter, probably trying to work out who I am. I do not linger. As I walk away I recall Tom saying to me recently, 'Once, I really believed that everything would stay the same forever. Didn't you?'

'Yes,' I replied, and tried to suppress a gasp of pain.

Tom is feeling browned off. He often gets like this in the village: it is too small a world for him now. I suppose it will always be home to him, because of the long stretch of time he spent here, growing through the years, but in young manhood he chafes against its various pettinesses. In such moods he fantasises wildly and humorously about what he would do if he were mayor. Today he outlines plans for the legalisation of marijuana and the establishment of a strip joint in the village square. As he is becoming more and more left-wing, he desires the speedy implementation of a rehabilitation programme for New Democracy voters and he sketches a plan whereby all leftovers from the junta, as he facetiously labels them, should be forced to donate fifty percent of their income to the Amalgamated Communist Writers' Union. 'Is there one?' I ask eagerly. 'No, but there will be,' is the firm reply. 'No man under the age of forty should be allowed to wear sunglasses, on the grounds that they look like potential dictators when they do.' It seems to escape him that this sort of edict is dictatorial behaviour.

Another departure day and I wake up with my mind a muddle of tags from literature and hymns: 'What were the use of my creation if I were entirely contained here? The whole universe would turn to a mighty stranger; I should not seem a part of it. Guide me, O thou great Jehovah, pilgrim through this barren land.' That sort of thing. I want to substitute 'foreign' for 'barren', and feel ill at the thought of restlessness and luggage. And ill at the thought of work, of reading to audiences, of being nerve-racked for the foreseeable future. And having to face loss yet again. For I am going to London and then on to Melbourne, where I have not been since the death of my mother.

But it is not time to move yet. It is eight o'clock in the morning and the Peloponnese, or at least this corner of it, is bathed in golden light. All my children are here, and all are still asleep. Jo and I were walking down the road last night when a bulky shadow, draped in packs both fore and aft, greeted us. It was Mick, who had been given some pre-election leave. He is full of tales to tell of poverty-stricken Armenian soldiers sent to train with the Greek army. They have to live on thirty dollars a month; they make little pipes out of battery cases and use tobacco they have pinched from nearby farms. When they are fortunate enough to have some cigarettes, they share them, sitting in a circle and puffing in turn. Electricity is available for only two hours a day in Armenia; there is a nuclear power plant in the area but the authorities are too scared to use it, lest it get bombed and cause a monumental disaster.

I hear frightening stories of Mick's commando training and am forced to look at photographs of him, a mere speck dangling from a great height over a vast expanse of water. Then there is the snakebite episode, during which one of his company got himself bitten. Mick was the only one with a snakebite kit, which sounded rather old-fashioned to me. He applied a tourniquet and then had to run six kilometres before he could manage to make radio contact. The victim was carried out on a stretcher and had to spend two days in hospital. Greece is not quite the same as Queensland. There are no taipans here.

A mad Athens, well even madder than usual, on election eve. A Greek-Australian once remarked to me that Athens has soul. Rhythm and blues, I wanted to say, I'm not so sure about the soul. But sometimes I manage to be tactful. Today, however, is fun, and I chuckle at the thought of what New Democracy voter G would say if he could see me tearing along the road to Melissia in a car draped with the green and white banners of PASOK, the Panhellenic Socialist Movement.

There are twenty-one parties fielding candidates. The Marxist-Leninists are still around in a vague sort of way, the Hunters' Party gets some attention, and there is a strangely named group called, as far as I can translate, the Greek Orthodox National Public Revolutionary Party. And a party for Hellenism, which I thought they all were automatically, whatever else they claim to be. How-to-vote leaflets are every-where (all those poor trees sacrificed), and lo, there is a spoof as well: there is a Mad party modelled on *Mad* magazine, with protagonist Alfred Newman appearing in various personae. It has always interested me that *Mad*, popular in Greece, is pronounced *Mud*.

It would be quite possible to spend one's whole life in England reading newspapers and doing nothing else. The latest input consists of samples of dottiness, mostly.

The award for the oddest book title of the year has been won by a tome called *Greek Rural Postmen and Their Cancellation Numbers*. I wonder briefly whether the said postmen know of this peculiar volume's existence. A previous winner was *Highlights in the History of Concrete*. Well, I've always said that titles are a great problem. While trying to choose a title for *A Stranger Here*, a process that did nothing for my tenuous grip on sanity, I decided that a couple of subtitles might be relevant: *Revenge* or *Messages to the Wilfully Obtuse*.

A man who was in court because he persisted in playing his bagpipes on Hampstead Heath, despite an ancient bylaw forbidding the playing of musical instruments there without written permission, maintained that the bagpipes were an instrument of war. The judge wryly remarked that the man's involuntary audience might well agree. The defence quoted the precedent of an unfortunate Highlander who was a piper for Bonnie Prince Charlie: he was hanged, drawn and quartered because his pipe was considered an instrument of war. Alas, the defendant lost his case, but remains defiant, saying that he will continue to play. 'They've got to catch me and I'm going to buy a fast bicycle.' With a pipe-carrier, I presume. That's the spirit.

OCTOBER

Don't tell anyone, but I have just bought myself a Scotch and ice at the bar in the Singapore airport transit lounge. There's a first time for everything, but it's hard to ignore the shake, rattle and roll of my ancestors' Presbyterian, very teetotal bones. Australian businessmen (and their accents bring tears to my eyes even before I start drinking the whisky) are lined up behind their Singapore Slings. But it is too late for me to become a bar baby, so I step up onto the marble floor and sink into the corner armchair near a potted palm.

Singapore airport glitters and shines. Even away from the rows of jewellery shops this is so: marble, perspex, steel, chrome, high-tech oily, wet-look plastic. Suddenly a Chinese pianist seats himself at the grand piano. The ebony surface is like a shaped pool; his gold-rimmed glasses, catching the light, glint and gleam; his head, sleek and black, merges with the piano more than once. He begins to play a jazzy rendition of 'Smoke Gets in Your Eyes' with a disgusting, jealousy-inducing ease, a stolid gaze and not even a sheet of music, drat him.

I wonder about the Chinese pianist. How much does he earn? Where does he go and what does he do when the evening's stint is over? Does he get any satisfaction at all out of seeing middle-aged women sitting tapping their feet in the lounge section of the travellers' bar? He is, I decide, as anonymous as I am.

The combination of anonymity and drink, as everybody knows, can produce outrageous impulses. My single impulse is not all that outrageous, I don't suppose: I merely want a dance partner. There is, after all, an inviting stretch of marble floor going to waste. But my impulse remains just that, for I am hardly the type to pick up a Singapore Slinging businessman, and in any case I am wearing rubber-soled shoes. And the inevitable jeans. I do not dress up for a 24-hour flight. Not any more.

The tune has changed and a rippling cascade of

notes breaks from agile fingers. 'No One Else Could Love You More'. Hmm. The melody finishes but there is no lingering on the part of the pianist. Loving you more doesn't include playing forever for an audience of one. The Scotch and I beam at him, and he nods graciously as he strolls off. Shortly afterwards I, too, stroll off – in the direction of the departure lounge, in the direction of Melbourne. Music and whisky have had little effect on the disquiet I feel at returning to the place I once called home.

I know I'm back in Melbourne when I'm given Grand Final news in the Tullamarine car park. But an interstate team is the victor. It's hard to remember the VFL any more, says my father sadly. All these other states. Television and radio don't tell you anything local. New South Wales is taking over the world.

But the world I knew has been taken over, anyway. I enter a transformed house and am poleaxed by pain. In a corner of the garden where nobody can see me, I become tearful. This house was once my mother's and is no longer. Twenty-four hours later, I emerge from the bowels of the underground at Melbourne Central and realise I am lost in La Trobe Street.

At night I start having restless dreams – again.

I'm lost, this time in a maze of school corridors. It's late and I cannot find the classroom, which is just as well because I'm wearing my nightdress. Time and again I meet a brick wall and set off once more along halls and passages, becoming increasingly exhausted, although an odd little section of my brain seems to be awake and intent on telling me that all this wandering is only a dream. In the end I am rescued by the obstetrician who delivered Mick.

It's strange how you miss a place more when you are actually in it. What you miss is the past, of course; you yearn for what was and can never be again. I think that's right, but am uncertain, as I am uncertain of so much now.

I soon stop getting lost and sit in suburban trains that might be, on occasion, threading their way through deep bush: the wattles are in full bloom and bronze-tipped gums shine in pale sunlight. It's spring in Melbourne and the sight of black-centred daisies growing alongside the railway track takes me back

forty-five years to a country childhood and the picking of daisies, to the making of chains which wilted
and withered all too soon in the heat.

Along Victoria's south-west coast the wattlebirds and
the New Holland honeyeaters are fussing, the ti-tree
is flowering in pinpoints of cream and white, and I try
to freeze the memory of the shifting bush shades of
green and grey, white and pink and brown, as a sort
of balance to the tossing of silver-green olive trees
and the towering, sculpted oaks and chestnuts of
mighty girth on the other side of the world. But the
beach of my childhood, an indentation on that long
shore, has changed, as sandstone will; a monolith has
toppled, as monoliths will, and the familiar landscape
is now blurred, by time as much as by weather. I
search for the child I was and find her gone forever;
nothing would induce my ageing self to scramble up
cliff faces and over rocky ledges the way she used to
do. Another loss.

The gaps are plugged by the Melbourne taxi driver who has me simmering with laughter at his black humour, a humour directed mainly against his father. 'Now *there's* a genuine racist. He thinks we should annexe New Zealand. "Yeah, son, we've given them a good chance and they've mucked it up, so we gotta step in, the sooner the better, and straighten out the mess and stop the rot." He seems never to have heard of the Treaty of Waitangi.' The taxi driver is a talented mimic. I tell him he should be on the stage, but he grins and says, 'Not me. My world's right here,' and a sweep of the hand indicates the interior of the cab. He is content with and within his theatre/world.

It is said that Barry Humphries gets a lot of his raw material as a result of riding in taxis in Australia. Well, it's difficult to chat to British taxi drivers, separated as they are from their passengers by their little glass walls. In Australia and in Greece I always sit in the front seat and I always learn a lot, as well as being able to keep an eye on the meter. So it is easy to believe that Humphries absorbs a great deal of comic material from a more democratic system, and the sheer variety of these people is an entertainment in itself. They come from the Sudan, from Russia, from Egypt, from everywhere. They write books. Don't ever tell a taxi driver you're a writer, warned my publisher. Too late. Not that a driver has ever wanted advice about the actual writing. No, they'd done all that and felt confident. What was next? That was the question. And how were they to get published? I sketched the procedure and wished them luck with both writing and driving.

I've had a driver who wrote Gothic fiction non-stop in his spare time, one who claimed he used to go to the races with Robert Holmes à Court, one who instructed me about Islam, and one who tried to teach me about the differences between the Coptic and the Greek Orthodox churches.

It is in Collins Street, in the shade of Scots Church, so much a part of my youth, that I recognise a face I have not seen for more than thirty years and have the courage to screech my delighted recognition. There is a reward: the face recognises mine. The people we have become then spend an hour traversing the vast space that divides us.

Later, other people bob up unexpectedly and carry me off to eat pasta and drink red wine in Carlton – at night, after pouring grey rain has ceased. The evening after rain means restaurant noise and velvet darkness sprinkled with the silvery hundreds-and-thousands of fairy lights in Lygon Street.

My uncle and I meet, again in Collins Street. He is a Western District farmer who will never live apart from his known world. Today he is kitted out in his uniform: corduroy trousers, tweed jacket, finely checked shirt, muted tie. The recurring cycle of fashion is too much for him.

'Will you look at that girl's bloomin' skirt? It's hardly a skirt at all.'

'You're the only man in Melbourne who's complaining.'

'I'm only thinking of the wool industry.'

'I bet.'

Three hours later we say goodbye. Pierced by a sadness which is, in part, a longing for simpler times and the recognition of an end to them, I wander changed streets and think that the best people do not, in essence, alter. I have just farewelled one of the straightest, most generous men I have ever known. Government and army propagandists could take his photo and mount it on a poster labelled 'The Spirit of Australia'.

Another dream. I am with an English friend on a Greek beach. We are having a picnic and she has made a cake. Quite suddenly and very heavily and deliberately, I place my bare foot on it. She is shocked. 'That's *awful*, what you've just done.' I know it is, cannot explain why I did it, and I *feel* awful. I spend the rest of our time trying, of course impossibly, to make amends. But there is no pretending it never happened, no pretending I never did it.

At least three times during these hectic weeks I meet strangers who say, staring, 'You're not at all what I expected.' When I ask them what they did expect, they do not want to answer, and so I am none the wiser. I have given up hope of being wise, in any case.

Uneasiness persists, and I fret over the various

disappearances, finding it hard to believe that Georges is closed – that establishment shop at which my sister, wearing the mandatory black dress and one piece of jewellery, had her first job, on handbags. Its windows, like so many hungry eyes, stare emptily onto the street. Once, men in pinstriped suits opened doors for country and Toorak matrons; there were always chairs next to the counters. In 1994 the Spencer Street Mail Exchange building was boarded up; now I do not even want to check to see what has happened to it.

The appearances and the alterations are no better. The casino is awful; its effects, social, moral and economic, are awful, and what would Melbourne's founding fathers have to say? Plenty. The problem of schools, hospitals, Albert Park, freeways, and the worry of some about the Asian presence are part of a world they could never have guessed at, as are maverick politicians and spokespersons whose only features are their big mouths. That precious commodity, grace, is conspicuously lacking. Whatever happened to good taste? Gone, all gone, along with Georges, white gloves and cucumber sandwiches. Of course the same has happened in other parts of the world, but, idiot that I am, I am able to tell myself that the changes there have nothing to do with me. The things that never change in Greece – nepotism, corruption, similar tomfoolery – are not my concern. So I deceive myself. So expatriates manage to protect themselves.

But the vibrations are here: you're elitist, you're ageing. Why did you leave? Why can't you stay? What is the matter with us? There is nothing more or less wrong with you: the problem is mine, because I have not been here to watch and cope with the slow accumulation of change, and the loss of security has been jolting and severe. Leaving was not my idea. Life sheers and veers off and carries individuals in different directions. As for coming back permanently, I don't think I can. Nothing stays the same, so the space I once occupied has closed over. Time has chipped away at the label on it – my name – and now I fear it has vanished forever.

I meet an unhappy woman. 'You've got haunted eyes,' I say boldly. 'I noticed them at once.'

'You've got them, too,' she replies slowly. 'That's the first thing I thought.'

I tell a friend, Ian, that I have been to a posh party where one of the guests, on discovering that I had a country childhood in a fairly remote part of the state, asked in hushed tones whether I had read or seen *Wake in Fright*. Which I haven't; obviously this is an important omission. Ian, as it happens, has seen it and takes deep offence. He, too, spent his childhood in a township.

'She's clearly the type who's never been further than Queenscliff in her life,' he remarks huffily.

'Come, come,' I say. 'Surely you mean Portsea?'

'Well, she needn't think that our place was anything like the scenes in *Wake in Fright*, because it wasn't, and isn't. I hate that sort of stereotyping, just hate it.'

'Calm down,' I say, but he does not listen.

'If she's not a product of Toorak, then she's a pastoralist's daughter who went to boarding-school and probably finishing-school as well. She could even have been presented at Court. God. I bet she can't even spell Yackandandah or Kinimikatka!'

I forbear to comment on the thorny subject of stereotyping, and fall to pondering the great Australian city–country divide, and then to wondering whether or not, depressing thought, class is not the greatest divide of all. My children accuse me of being an outrageous, colossal snob, and say they thought Australians were not supposed to admit that the word 'class', let alone the concept, exists. So then I remind myself and them that Manning Clark considered the great chasm to fall between those who mock and those who mourn. Guiltily, I have occasionally thought that if my father had been a shearer or a timber-cutter, and I had had the tough life that went with such occupations, I would have been much more fitted for life in the Peloponnese and would not have felt compelled to be polite at all costs, would not have tried so hard to please. My mother-in-law and I might have carved out some sort of genuine relationship if I had been prepared to fight her in her own way.

But it wasn't as simple as that, was not a matter of just being prepared. My temperament is not a combative one, and my conditioning also meant that I simply couldn't fight – my parents, both teachers, came from a generation in which teachers were responsible not only for the transmission of knowledge, culture, citizenship and patriotism, but also for an insistence on certain standards of good behaviour and manners. That these last were very much dependent on a narrow definition and on what men and religion approved of did not occur to me for a very long time.

In the Melbourne General Cemetery, walking along curving paths on my way to visit friends in North Carlton, and charting the different sections – Greek Orthodox; Roman Catholic, with old Labor stalwarts featuring prominently – I come across a tomb inscribed 'Requested in Peace'. It's nice to think that God is not too demanding or aggressive, that even He has to mind His manners in Melbourne. I laugh and remember the death notice inserted by a woman whose deceased mother-in-law had driven her mad for twenty-five years: 'Peace at Last'.

Near the university I catch a glimpse of a girl who could have been me thirty years ago, in that she is the same physical type. She is following the same route I took to lectures way back then. But I never strode along in trousers, never tossed my hair the way she is tossing hers now. Worse luck. Those were the days of straight skirts, Hush Puppies, angora twinsets, the fake pearl necklace bought by Granny in Coles, the tortures of rollers and hairspray, stockings and suspender belts. The first time I ever wore trousers in public was when I went rushing down to the corner of Elizabeth Street and Flemington Road in order to get a glimpse of The Beatles as their car crept along fan-clogged roads on its way from the airport to the Southern Cross Hotel. (My children are impressed by my boast of having seen The Beatles, but when I tell them I rushed to see President Johnson, too, in 1966, they say, Who?)

Amy, born in England, resident in Australia, herself a migrant, says that migrants can only create an identity if they carry and hold their memories. These memories are a cardboard box to sleep in whenever migrants consider themselves to be homeless. But for this small interval I am safely in the present and even feel at home, though I know the feeling will not last, and I become manic with glee at being in a familiar world, a familiar book world, at meeting my friends and making new ones, even if they are only temporary. My opus gets launched and I feel relieved that it is between covers, on shelves and presumably being read, at least by some people. My mother's friends come to see me, talk about her, bring her close again, although she is never far away. And I have a temporary identity here; well, I think I have. The softness of the southern spring soothes me, rubs balm into the wounds of change.

The night before I leave Australia I have a nightmare. As usual. I am a big Chinese doll, dressed in red satin. I have no feet, but am fixed instead on some sort of roller and being propelled forward at tremendous speed. There is a dagger in my hand and I am hurtling towards a set of red satin curtains, which open suddenly, allowing me to stab, with great force, an exposed torso.

The pattern is repeating itself: same airport and bar, same chair and drink. But I have a sense of unfinished business for more reasons than one. Somewhere I have read or heard that Daniel Defoe considered that mobility produced guilt; Nathaniel Hawthorne, on the other hand, blamed stasis. Guilt, clearly, is the thing, and not to be escaped, not even in the space between responsibilities provided by transit lounges.

I ponder the guilt that accompanies leaving, returning, staying for a short time then leaving again, but part of me is still looking down at the Australia unrolling thirty thousand feet below, part of me is still being worked on by the spell of place. No wonder, when the terrain changes from trees tracing watercourses to squares of settlement merging from green to sand to brown, when organised space gives way to dusty desert marked by furrows or the tucks and pleats of mountain ranges. Here and there a thread of water gleams, and in the north-west, below the cotton-wool puffs of cloud, I see mother-of-pearl water bordering a coastline.

But what passes for reality is here and now. A little girl (perhaps she is six, perhaps not that old) is standing at the same grand piano and picking out the tune of 'Twinkle, Twinkle, Little Star'. After a few minutes the same Chinese pianist ambles up and delights the child and quite a few other people by playing several versions of the nursery rhyme. Once again, he makes the trills, runs, ripples and cascades of complicated, entrancing variations seem ridiculously easy, and, the ageing brain being what it is, I am reminded of the old nonconformist hymn for children: 'In this world of darkness/So we must shine/You in your small corner and I in mine.'

I am not shining in my corner of the transit lounge. Not at all. I pick up my bag and head for yet another departure lounge and for another place which is home and not home. Fourteen hours later, stars pierce the darkness over London as the plane touches down.

Mohammed is supposed to have said, 'A journey is a fragment of Hell.' I think it was Paul Scott who wrote that every departure, every goodbye, is a rehearsal of death.

November

London, too, is a space between responsibilities.
During the long periods I spend here, the resident
puritan in my psyche gives me a hard time, muttering
about self-indulgence: Shame on you, he hisses. (The
puritan is definitely masculine, and very probably a
Presbyterian minister.)

At Heathrow the Irish bus conductor admires my
Akubra hat and announces he has friends living at
Eltham, in Melbourne. The bus moves slowly through
west London and I tell myself that the bare trees of
Kensington Gardens, creating gaps and spaces, are not
enough to look at after the leafy fullness of Melbourne
in the spring, and the trees are all wrong, anyway.
There is a nip of frost in the air; I emerge from the bus

into it, and feel very cold, not just because of the weather. I am morose from jet-lag and goodbyes and fear. Fear because of the question, What's next? I am a feminine incarnation of Mr Micawber, but dread that the 'something will turn up' philosophy may eventually prove to be a hollow one, a snare and a delusion. I fear the risk, I fear the uncertainty; both these things and the fear itself are expanding and worsening – one of the effects of ageing. Most of all I fear that my complicated griefs will one day overwhelm me.

But I don't know what else to do except keep on the way I am going. 'You're living life by default,' said an academic friend when I told him this. 'Thanks,' I said. 'I know.'

What am I to do about it? I asked myself, not him. I am slightly reassured by the thought of a snippet I read recently, one which clarified the parable of the talents. I have always worried about this parable, thinking it an endorsement of capitalism, and have always had a sneaking sympathy with the servant who buried his talent in the back yard. Years ago the sight of an actual talent in the Heraklion Museum confirmed this sympathy, as they happen to be quite large and would have taken a lot of digging and burying. But the snippet I read suggested that burying the talent in the garden is the riskiest thing one can do, and really means the burying of the chance of growth, development, life. Something like that. I feel reassured because now I understand that my Marxist interpretation was not the right one. Talents of whatever sort must be used.

The resident puritan also chides me for my restlessness and a lot else besides. I quote Robert Louis Stevenson to him: 'The untented Kosmos my abode, I pass, a wilful stranger.' And 'To travel hopefully is a better thing than to arrive.' And 'The true success is to labour.' That lot ought to shut him up, at least for a while. (I try not to think about the disparity between amounts of labour and degrees of success.)

Guy Fawkes' Day, and in previous years here I have seen the groups of small children wheeling stuffed, homemade dummies around in battered prams while reiterating the Penny for the Guy message, which I had never heard before. Some parts of ritual drop off or get lost when they are transplanted, but in country Victoria all that time ago we certainly had a most magnificent bonfire every year, helped along by the rubber tyres that I now cringe to think about, and by spectacular fireworks: the whirling, falling dazzle of Catherine wheels has taken a long time to fade in the memory. St Catherine was supposed to have met her death early in the fourth century by being put upon a wheel resembling a chaff-cutter. But the moment the wheel began to turn, her bonds were miraculously broken; her persecutors, who resented not only her spirited defence of the Christian faith but her apparent indestructibility, took no chances and had her beheaded. I did not know these things when I was seven, which was probably just as well, having been possessed of a somewhat morbid imagination.

I do not go out on Guy Fawkes' night; I hear an occasional cracker in the street and that is all. The double-bungers let off at Greek Easter are enough for me; I invariably stuff cotton wool in my ears, but still jump with fright at every detonation. Had I been my grandfather and in the trenches of France I would have been an early candidate for shell-shock. He managed to last four years, God knows how.

I suppose I am becoming detribalised, but only slowly, because quintessentially Australian rituals still interest me more than occasions like bonfire night. Australians all acknowledge that on the first Tuesday in November there is only one event worth thinking about, and that is a certain horserace. It doesn't matter too much where you happen to be, either. I blush to confess that I have never actually been to the event, but I can boast of having been to the next best thing, which is the Melbourne Cup Night do at the Australian Embassy, Athens.

The average Aussie taxpayer will be reassured to know that preparations for this wing-ding start weeks ahead of time, when diplomatic wives and other assorted mortals are dragooned into taking part in the Great Lamington Bash. It would do Dame Edna's heart good to see dedicated females slaving over Australia's afternoon-tea icon. At the end of this session square metres of lamington are consigned to freezers all over Athens, pending the great night: the ritual cutting, chocolate icing and coconut rolling require a further session of intensive labour at the last minute. The good old meat pie is also present in vast quantities: one year, when flights from Australia, or the lack of them, were a problem, the embassy in Rome stood by with dry ice and all necessary contingency arrangements.

Then there is the field to be considered, for actual races, albeit with wooden horses, take place, and programmes are printed. Weighty matters, such as civil conflicts and the injustice of Greek-Australian youths being forced to do Greek national service, are forgotten as the great and the good forgather on many a late night to list runners like 'Newcomer, by Old Hand out of Hilton Rendezvous: a very promising filly. Shows great staying power over the distance.'

Picture the scene: all floors of the embassy are decorated to the last square inch with Australiana: trails of gumleaves, sprigs of wattle, racing paraphernalia of all kinds, flags, beer cans of essential brands, bales of hay, you name it. Everybody who is anybody is there, and the uninhibited take part in the Hat Parade. Your humble correspondent does her best with a jockey cap decorated (sort of) with miniature Australian flags; possum, kanga and emu pins; and a silver-foil horseshoe or two. Purloined gumleaves help.

An embassy official, eyeing this creation, says, 'Something's missing, love. Be right with ya,' and

produces a clip-on koala which he attaches precari-
ously to a drooping bit of eucalyptus. One man,
speaking broad Strine which is music to my ears, looks
thoughtfully at my headgear and announces, 'Now,
that's a winner. Dunno that I like it, but it's definitely
a winner.' It isn't, alas.

Lest the upper echelons of Athenian society think
we are an uncultured mob, an opportunity to study
ancient history (well, ancient by Australian standards)
is provided: television sets show footage of what seems
like every Melbourne Cup ever run. Bill Collins (who
else?) narrates. There are raffles with sumptuous
prizes, and serious money is involved in those mysterious transactions known as the Trifecta and the
Quadrella. Everybody eats and drinks a lot. Fashions
of the field may not equal Flemington standards but
are not bad, all the same.

Come the start of the race programme and the
Greek-Australian Mistress of Ceremonies, patriotically
wearing a gorgeous cartwheel of a black hat that her
mother bought in Georges, Melbourne, in 1949, produces two huge rubber dice. Jockeys line up with their
wooden horses. One die selects which horse is to move,

the other how many moves it is permitted to make along the truncated track marked out on the embassy floor. Excitement runs high: the noise of barracking in a confined space is deafening, and sighs of defeat and disappointment reach gale force at the end of each event.

The night wears on and many people wear out. My hat, denuded steadily of its mini-flags by sentimental Greek-Australians, is bald by the end of the night. A Greek-Australian man has the last word: 'Jeez, it was almost as good as the real thing, *paithaki mou!*'

Snow – which I hadn't even realised was falling until I got out the front door. Now, at lunchtime, the weather situation has improved or deteriorated, depending on your point of view, and the snow has stopped, but at half past nine this morning, silly old me, I felt as if I were walking along in the middle of an expanded and very traditional Christmas card. I don't imagine the great British public felt the same way; they were trudging along with the glumly stoic look which is so characteristic. 'They're all at least mildly depressed, the Brits,' observed an Australian friend recently. 'No bloody wonder, it's the greyness.' The thought occurs to me that my sisters-in-law suffer from the same sort of depression on catching a glimpse of my hair.

But a Chinese girl in Haverstock Hill was grinning from ear to ear. I was not as delighted, concentrating as I was on not falling over in the street, but I thought, Oh well, another experience and one that Jo would give his eye-teeth for. I tested my fourth-grade teacher's assertion that snowflakes look like black feathers while they are falling. Looking up and getting an eyeful, I decided to make that grey feathers instead.

The festive ordeal seems to begin earlier and earlier every year. Of course I've missed the last day for sending Christmas cards to Australia by surface mail. (Most of these get sent airmail by mistake anyway.) In a shop at Swiss Cottage a young male assistant is wearing a set of red-and-green reindeer's antlers. 'Do you get penalty rates for wearing those?' I ask, but he ignores this facetious remark. I also note that it is possible to obtain antlers that light up and play music.

Festivity, so-called, continues at a mega-shopping

centre, one of the most refined instruments of torture devised by modern person. These are temples of consumerism where, strange to say, one often has to work like a dog or a galley-slave in order to make the most basic purchase. In passing I note a woman who has green hair the precise shade of her anorak; I wonder what the sisters-in-law would say to that? And in one of the very large shops a salesman is wearing a label which says, 'I speak Greek.' I do not put this announcement to the test.

Then I stumble on Santa's Grotto. Not into it, thank God. It is a towering, multi-layered edifice of sparkle, tinsel and perambulating fairytale figures which would make any self-respecting toddler possessed of the smallest degree of imagination scream blue murder. A teenage girl, clearly hired for this season so favourable to Mammon, wears a surreal outfit consisting of a mulberry-coloured top, striped tights, and filmy, diaphanous wings somehow attached to her back. Small queues are already forming. Been there, done that: in Camberwell Road, Melbourne, and it was hot, and two little boys, Tom and Mick, were wearing on that long-ago day shirts with prophetic labels: 'Kalamata, Greece'. Women lose a whole world when they have a baby, because they can never be free again, but they gain another world, one that both entertains and torments with its unpredictability. Perhaps I have gained too many worlds; perhaps that is what migration, as well as childbirth, does.

Overwhelmed by nostalgia and ashamed that such materialism has stimulated it, I flee, and much against my expectations find a familiar car in the most enormous car park I have ever seen. I now have a deeper understanding of David Livingstone et al, feeling as if I have just conquered a desert or mapped a dangerous coast, contending all the while with threatening tribes.

To the Heath on a blue-bright afternoon. The sky, for reasons I do not understand, has a yellow rim and the buildings of London are sharp in the still, grey pollution cloud. Kites are soaring high; squirrels are bounding about. Every so often the latter stop short, looking like religious old women with their hands clasped while they gaze and meditate.

A mad but satisfying day spent at full gallop. Work in the morning, meeting a deadline: the fear that I will not be able to meet a deadline never leaves me. To a long lunch at a beautiful, large, stylish South Kensington flat where I feel, above all, comfortable, because I am in Australian company. I do not have to puzzle over the signals, because I know them. There is a shorthand in the conversation that there can never be with people of other cultures. I feel my manners are comprehensible and acceptable; this is the way I feel in Australia, but not, at least not very often, in London or the Peloponnese.

Manners are important, as I keep insisting to Tom, Mick and Jo. The trouble is that when you are a migrant manners become much more important, because you are never sure where you are with them. There is little universality about manners. I have spent a lifetime assuming that good manners consist in making other people feel comfortable; in Europe this is far from the truth. Manners seem so often a weapon, very subtly deployed, in the campaign to prove effortless superiority. Perfect manners are a perfect way to keep somebody at arm's length. The British say, Do keep in touch, and then are surprised and more than a little affronted when you take them at their word. They also say, We must have dinner, or, You must come over. I know certain Australians who would immediately produce their diaries; I have managed to avoid this gaffe. Well, at least that's one.

Migrants are literal-minded, particularly when operating in a language not their own. In Greece piecrust promises are a way of life. Many an event, party, social gathering I expected has never come to pass. I took a long time to learn about taverna talk, during which you might be promised the world; more fool you if you expect to take delivery. 'You get your heart set on things,' G has said accusingly many times. 'No, I don't,' I have replied, also many times. 'I just like to know what's happening.' Australian manners combine openness and a casual attitude that bewilders Europeans, who seem entirely unable to cope with the 'let's make it up as we go along' way of approaching social interaction. I am an Australian and automatically assumed to be casual, but I still wish there could be a water jug on the speakers' table at Australia House instead of a plastic bottle.

I feel like the Africans I once heard of who were in a boat for the first time, seeing the sea for the first time, and who were bewildered. Where are the tracks? they kept wanting to know. Precisely my question when it comes to the dangerous, unknown territory of manners.

At a BBC taping, I am a member of the audience but also an acquaintance of the producer. I blot my copybook later by being over-helpful. Manners again. Asked to stay on after the taping is over, I quite automatically start to roll up yards of lead and flex. Do you work here? asks a panellist in a far from friendly manner. No, I say, and then reflect on the various voices that have led to my giving this impression.

The old puritan: earn your keep and you might have a faint hope of justifying your existence.

The ageing mother, conditioned by her own mother: there's always something to be done. Do it.

The quasi-Greek peasant: work, work, work, or else what will people say? And we might all starve to death unless you, the woman, keep on.

Too late I realise that this unmotivated, automatic

helpfulness might be construed as an attempt to ingra-
tiate myself. Fat chance. I'm just not very good at
standing around doing nothing.

My nights are restless and my dreams easily inter-
preted. I am at a grand party in a posh flat in London.
Very surprisingly, the party is for me, given by a person
on whom I dote and to whom I would like to be
necessary. He, however, does not wish to acknowledge
something as simple as a continued and straightforward
preoccupation of affection. Safe in his role as host, he
never comes near me, but waits hand and foot on his
other guests. The flat is huge and I simply wander about
it; I wander so long and so far that quite soon, in the
manner of dreams, I find myself back in leafy
Melbourne, in Alexandra Avenue with the Yarra flowing by. But then, just as suddenly, I am back in London,
standing at the window of a building opposite the place
where the party is still going on. I catch glimpses of the
host, still being the social animal supreme, but I
glimpse him from afar, and through glass.

Always from afar and always through glass, always

the indifference; I appeal in vain. Some people clank around in invisible suits of armour; some people, always strategists, resolve never to engage in unguarded friendship. Keats wrote to Fanny Brawne; 'I am greedy of you . . . Do not live as if I was not existing.' Mary Wollstonecraft was often more temperate, and said she liked the word 'affection', because it signified something habitual. A friend of mine, my own age, asked her mother not too long ago when the whole awful business of love and desire, rejection and pain stops. Mother eyed daughter carefully and then said, 'When I find out, I'll let you know.' She was eighty-two.

I wake up thinking of Robert Louis Stevenson again: 'There is no duty we so much underrate as the duty of being happy.' It has taken me about forty years to work out what Oscar Wilde meant when he said that happiness is no laughing matter, and I am none the better for now knowing: sometimes I wish I had never learned that loneliness is not compulsory. I had a plain girl's faith in a happy ending, was taught to believe that hard work and an iron will and consistent good behaviour and regular prayer, as a type of recipe or spell, would get me anything I wanted, that if I behaved justly I would be treated justly. Crammed full of hope, religion and ethics as I was, it took me a long time to learn that God sometimes reserves the right to say no, that people in general are unpredictable and that the most important person in one's life can be the most unpredictable of all. I had to learn, very slowly and painfully, that the world was not made for me. It is all so obvious, but I am a full-time student in some sort of remedial class for the immature, apparently quite unable to graduate, and have spent time recently pondering George Eliot's remark that the happiest women, like the happiest nations, have no history.

A terrible plague is afflicting English. It has been called Greengrocer's Apostrophe, but it is so highly contagious that other retailers are becoming infected, with the result that literate consumers are suffering. Signs bristle with messages like the following: *Bargain Potato's* and *Golden Deliciou's*. To my mingled joy and sorrow I saw *Legging's 5 pounds* recently. There is another blight as well, and that is the spreading practice of enclosing various words and phrases quite unnecessarily in inverted commas. It grieves me to have to report that grand estate agents are not immune, for lately I have read advertisements in very glossy magazines: *Very desirable property for sale 'In the heart of Knightsbridge.' Excellent opportunity available in 'Knightsbridge Village'*. Things have come to a pretty pass, and where will it all end? Shopkeepers' signs are in general fascinating: my notebook reminds me of one I saw in Mousehole, Cornwall: *Due to feeding of gulls Beware They are now stealing <u>ice-cream</u>*. That last full stop is mine, all the sign-writer's punctuating energy having gone into the capital letters, and an underline for emphasis.

As I emerge from the divine ambience of Hatchard's in Piccadilly, wondering whether it would be possible to stow away in a book shop rather than in the House of Lords, I see a kilted Scot across the street. I whizz my glasses on even more quickly than I did the night I saw a mouse run across the dining-room floor at the Royal Overseas League. At least that happened after dinner. 'Stop squeaking, Mildred,' I upbraided my companion. 'Leave that to the mouse.' I've been fairly blasé about mice ever since one ran across my face and woke me up. That was years ago in Australia. On another occasion a cat of doubtful lineage and I (we were well matched when it came to lineage) hunted a mouse out from underneath a seventeenth-century oak bed in a Holland Park house. Since then mice have built nests under my Peloponnesian sink and elsewhere, but I will admit to feeling a frisson when I saw a grey tail hanging out of Jo's toybox.

But I digress, and feel another frisson as I gaze, while trying to pretend I'm not gazing, at this tall vision in Black Watch. It's my ancestors, I tell myself. Liar. It's the swing of the hips, the broad shoulders, the ramrod-straight back, the steel-grey hair under the Glengarry, the charm of, well, everything, but most of all it's the shapely legs covered in tight-fitting socks. Men and their legs. It's just as well I was not born in the eighteenth century or before, with all those fashions involving silk hose and buckled shoes. I would never have got any work done. Covered legs are much more appealing than bare ones, of course.

But this is no way to spend the day, and is hardly dignified in one whose way of life has fallen into the sere and yellow leaf. There are certain things I must not look to have. Also, I tell myself, this man, while handsome and extremely stylish, probably has a wife and six children towards whom he is patriarchal and unpleasant, particularly at breakfast-time. Even if we were to meet and he were to charm me, it would not be difficult to remind myself that charm is so often like the rainbow film on the surface of a dank pool. Then again, and very importantly, I cannot catch a glimpse of his knees. Knobbly, prob'ly.

I turn towards the tube station and consider not only men's legs, but the way they walk. Not far ahead of me I can see a Greek man. Even with his head in a bag, I would have known him for a Greek because of the way he moves: there is a swagger of the hips, quite different from the Scot's swing, although both move-ments are clearly related to the wearing of the *fustanella* and the kilt. The Greek walk is an arrogant, show-offy, 'look at me, all females present, and eat your hearts out', sort of walk. Australian men simply cannot be bothered with all that; I don't think Englishmen can, either. The Australians favour a relaxed cross between a lounge and a lope, although you can always tell an Australian Rules rover by his jauntier method of perambulation. Englishmen have a brisk and slightly ducklike gait: their feet tend to splay outwards at the very moment their knees are knocking together, which is possibly symbolic and definitely ungraceful. It resembles the gangle of the perennial and languid adolescent who might be tempted onto a croquet lawn once a year if the incentive (strawberries? champagne?) is great enough.

Speakers' Corner. Quite a crowd is here, but things are not as lively as they might be, possibly because of some rather serious rain. So often rain in London is of the light, misty, drizzling, annoying sort. Three speakers are addressing those who care to listen. One is advocating world government, another is deploring the state of the nation, and the third is trying to save us all for Jesus. (Nothing changes very much, in spite of what we all like to think.)

'The Devil,' this last roundly declares, 'is a cheat, a liar and a pervert.'

'Just the sort of man I like,' ripostes a man in the crowd, twirling a striped umbrella by way of emphasis.

'If Heaven's such a great place, what are you waiting for?' screeches another. 'Don't hang about.'

It was November when I left Greece some years ago, swearing never to go back. I wandered about Athens, imagining, no, really believing, that I was saying goodbye to 'the divine, violet-crowned and shining city,' or what was left of it. Of course I was wrong. Saying goodbye is a huge problem which I am quite unable to solve.

My sister did not like goodbyes, either. The last one, in Melbourne, was very painful. I told her I would soon be back. But then she died, suddenly and by her own hand, leaving a will but no note. And now I am left with the pain of that last unsatisfactory goodbye. And all the things I wanted to say will remain unsaid forever, while she has exercised the privilege of an intentionally endless silence.

Recently I read something about death involving not just the disappearance of a person, but also the death of hope, memory and feeling. My hopes died for other reasons; my memory is fairly intact. So far. My feeling for my sister is just the same, and I do not imagine that it will disappear or change with the passing of time. What I have lost, apart from her physical presence, is a sense of a shared past. Childhood within the family has gone forever, because there is no one to talk it over with.

My brother was too young when we left the township to recall the sights of the place where my sister and I spent so many formative years: the clouds of cockatoos; the golden waves of wheat and the surrounding flatness punctuated by the thin fingers of the silos; the thick gatherings of merinos in the never-ending paddocks; the gardens with the Black Boy roses, sunflowers, lantana bushes, the red and yellow cannas at the front of houses and the spreading cantaloupes and purpling globes of Nelly Kelly passionfruit vines out the back. He cannot remember the sounds of the steam trains and the noisy dawns of the opening of the duck-shooting season. He cannot hope to recall the skirling of the pipes at the football matches and at the Royal Agricultural Shows; he was not even born when we donned our costumes for a suitably patriotic display at the time of the Coronation, and was only a baby when we rose, in high excitement, at the crack of dawn to put on our white organdie frocks and set off by steam train in order to glimpse the Royal Couple for fully two minutes. He could not read when we left, by which time we had given up reading Phantom comics and Schoolgirls' Own Library and had tired of the sight of Mandrake gesturing hypnotically.

My sister was a lioness for others, but was, ultimately, unable to help herself. In the beginning she had everything – looks, charm, intelligence, a beautiful singing voice – but at the end there was nothing but the terrible blankness of complete despair. And at the end she did not have the strength even to say goodbye. I am able to go back to Greece, but I can no longer visit my sister.

DECEMBER

December's bareness. When I first came to London it was with such a sense of relief that I believed the freezings and the dark days were over. Such confidence did not last; I realised eventually that appearances in a new country are always of a strictly provisional nature. However, it was a sound move, psychologically speaking, to come here and to try to be something other than a tourist, to make a sideways shift to a place and society that was both familiar and strange, to attempt to replace the drama of village life with the fantasy of a great city.

I should have been doing all this thirty years before, but then I always was a late developer. When I was single I did not travel, at least not very much, but

then I was not single for very long, not by today's standards, at any rate. I will be back in Greece for
Christmas; it is nearly twenty years since I had a southern, hot Christmas. But in Victoria now the jacarandas
will be in bloom, and the gums will be blossoming
red: sitting here in frosty Hampstead it does not take
much to imagine the scent of eucalyptus.

Fate, with its usual quirks, leads me to be involved with
the dismantling of an old woman's life. The
widowed and childless Mrs Bourke has reached the
stage at which she can no longer look after herself and
has to leave the small flat which has been her home for
at least thirty years. She fits the classic pattern
of the aged of a certain background, regardless of
country. Poverty and frugality are very hard habits
to break, become revered and enshrined – as if they
constitute or lead to a kind of nobility, instead of a
grinding insensitivity as so often happens – and I can't
help thinking that Christianity, or at least the sort I was
raised on, with its emphasis on self-sacrifice, has a lot
to answer for. It seems to me that women have always

had to make the most sacrifices, and were carefully and consistently conditioned to think that they did not deserve anything much in the way of comfort. In Mrs Bourke's flat there is no carpet, virtually no heating, no phone, and only a few tins of peas and tuna in the pantry. Yet she has quite a lot of money in the bank.

But then, G's uncle did not know how to spend his old age pension, I recall. What a lot of money, he would say of the paltry amount. What am I going to do with it all? Yiayia would always use a match twice, using the fire to light the match she needed for her gas ring. All the plastic bags she collected were torn into long strips which she then crocheted into circular mats. My grandmother kept a cache of pound notes under sheets of newspaper on the bottom of her wardrobe. They were found after her death: her savings from the housekeeping money.

Both my grandmothers were forced to leave school at fourteen. Their fathers forbade them to work: when my spirited and defiant maternal grandmother got herself a job as a window-dresser, her father followed her to the shop, ranted and raged in a manner which was apparently all too familiar, and brought her home. I like to think that she put up a good fight. She certainly fought a running battle with her father when he tried to arrange a marriage for her; it took her a long time to win, but she eventually married the man of her choice. My paternal grand-mother, equally spirited but not as oppressed, was permitted to accompany her brother, a Presbyterian minister, on his missionary work in Western Australia.

They were frustrated women, my grandmothers, with their undoubted intelligence cramped and thwarted. Yet, with their attachment to religion, their voracious reading habits, their wide range of interests and subversive senses of humour, they managed to do their domestic duty and enjoy life at the same time. My mother came from a similar mould: they looked about them, these women, and felt themselves to be happy.

I do not feel myself to be happy when I see old village women in church. Greek villages are a statistician's and a demographer's dream, conforming to all the established graphs and patterns. They are places inhabited largely by the old and the ageing; because men marry women ten or more years younger there are many widows, old before their time, wearing the complete black which relentlessly crushes any vestige of remaining youth. A fortunate widow has her children and grandchildren to console her, but one of the unfortunates, eighty-year-old Kyria Persephone, recently bereaved, wept when I stopped one afternoon to exchange a few words. She has no children, and takes no joy in the company of her sister.

'She has her children,' she remarked bitterly. 'What have I got? Now that my husband is dead, I want to die, too.'

This is not the way Kyria Persephone is supposed to think or feel. The Christian Orthodox religion is supposed to be the consolation surpassing all others. For many old women it is: every Sunday they can be seen, gaunt faces under their headscarves, gazes fixed on the priest, their lips moving as the *psaltoi* chant. When the Great Procession begins, they lower themselves creakingly to the floor and make the sign of the Cross in great sweeping movements as the elements are presented to the congregation. I have yet to observe a man doing this, although there is much punctilious bowing of male heads, and automatic, if cramped, sketching of the Cross with the requisite three fingers.

When I look at these women and reflect on their hard lives, so lacking in light-hearted pleasure or even minimal comfort, and with little to hope for except a *kalos thanatos* – a good death – I do not feel happy. I do not feel Christian. I feel angry. What has God ever done for them? I ask myself, and wait for the thunderbolt. I would, of course, never dare ask them, any more than I would have asked my grandmothers the same question. Perhaps the answers I guess at would be the same from grandmothers and the old Greeks: God has shown them how to get through life without repining, has provided them with the security of certainty, and has made them aware of the mysterious and the miraculous, even enabling them to participate in both. Envy should replace my anger.

A tree has been felled in Haverstock Hill and a huge hollow gapes in the stump. Soon a couple of signs appear. One says simply, 'Why?' And another says, 'The lengths people will go to to get a Christmas tree.' And a little later bunches of flowers are placed there in memory of the tree.

Outside the tube station another sign: 'A bandicoot is for life, not just for Christmas.' There is a number to ring which will put the conscientious and concerned in touch with the Bandicoot Protection Society. I am tempted to write the number down but feel too foolish to do so; even if I memorise it I know I will never ring it, although it would be fun to find out who the mad Australian is. Well, who the other one is.

Out to dinner with two doctors and a designer, and I become fascinated by the differences in vocabulary and modes of expression. 'On drinking even a small amount of red wine,' announces one doctor, 'my wife presents the following physiological symptoms,' and he lists them all in detail, finishing with a return to standard speech, 'and then she falls asleep.' We are having a Chinese meal and he solemnly intones, 'Microbiologically speaking, boiled rice is much safer than fried.' As one who never speaks microbiologically at all, I am interested in this handy piece of information. Of course I much prefer fried rice; well, I would, wouldn't I?

The designer leans towards me and scrutinises my ears closely. Somewhat to my alarm. 'It's all right. I'm just trying to establish the provenance of your earrings. Australia or Greece?'

'Australia,' I reply, wondering why 'Where did your earrings come from?' is not a satisfactory question to ask. But then academics make allusions, have their own form of jargon, while writers and mighty readers are often accused of speaking in an excluding sort of way, practising a kind of verbal intertextuality which others find hard to follow. Nobody can help these habits, which are simply the accretions of age and a way of life. It has to be admitted, however, that I generally revel in the way the English speak and play with language: the quotations, the anecdotes, the aphorisms, the labyrinth of subordinate clauses through which they wander with the certainty of a Theseus who has no doubt whatsoever in the efficacy and strength of Ariadne's thread, the irony, the dry humour, the understatements. And the love of the extended simile and metaphor.

I seem to remember that Wittgenstein considered that one's world is limited by the limits of one's language. For some people there is no limit to either.

Some writers consider that all writers are manic-depressives. I don't know. What I do know is that the black dog is sniffing at my heels again; he seems to know the secret anniversaries of my heart. As long as he doesn't decide to go for my throat I'll be all right. Dr Johnson hoped always to resist his black dog, which barked constantly at him from breakfast until dinner-time, and then visited him again at night. I get tired of resisting, and simply wish I could feed the animal a cyanide tablet. But company helps to fend him off; he doesn't like company, doesn't like to hear me wise-cracking my way through this vale of tears. I put on my cap and bells, although these are occasionally replaced by the prickles and quills of the porcupine, but then there comes the point when the company departs or I depart: at that moment the restlessness and sense of futility descend once more. Like the fall of a curtain, like the settling of a blanket.

I huddle under the blanket of futility and ask myself what I am doing in a place where I am an observer and only that. I have no family here, not a single relative or connection, at least not one that I know of, although there are almost certainly some third cousins somewhere in Scotland. But it is only in Greece that third cousins count. My writing is affected by my observer status, I consider; I do not write about Britain in the same way that I write about Greece and Australia. One reason for this is a kind of inhibition which comes from being both knowledgeable and ignorant about this mysterious place. I am not involved, despite my wishes, to the necessary degree. I made my move too late.

I'm at Gatwick again and becoming maudlin at the thought that I'm measuring out my life in departure lounges. Helpful friends declare that every problem has a solution, but it ain't necessarily so. Years ago now, when Jo came to England and I was giving him treats galore, we went to a film called *Into the West*, which I mistakenly thought was a Western. Instead it was a tear-jerker about two orphaned Irish gypsy children and their grief-stricken father. I staggered out of the cinema with red eyes and Jo was disgusted with me. The father in the film memorably remarks, 'There's a bit of the traveller in all of us, and very few of us know where we're going.' Well, I do and I don't.

What I do know is that I am an outsider returning to a particular place and community; what I do know is that in anthropology the outsider is both dangerous and in danger. These subjects have exercised many minds and have produced varying opinions. Patrick White wrote about the disease of foreignness and how a foreigner in Greece is always a bit of a joke. Angela Carter, on the other hand, said that alienated is the only way to be. But settled people resent gypsies, people who believe in action are wary of observers, and a great many people have an innate disapproval of untidiness. My life is, more than anything else, untidy, and several people would like me to do something about this continuing state of affairs; unfortunately for them, my metaphor for living has never been that of the filing-cabinet. At least, I tell myself, movement reassures me that I'm still alive: there is, after all, not much room for movement in a grave, and plenty of time to rest.

I feel like having a good cry but the effort seems too much, people will stare at me, and anyway, the flight has been delayed two hours in the middle of the night, so that my eyes are going to be quite bloodshot enough by the time I arrive in Athens. I concentrate instead on the counter-culture girls who are off to Athens or other destinations with their Greek boyfriends. The skulls of these girls gleam and match the shine of the several rings inserted into various facial parts: ears, noses, eyebrows. One is wearing a tattered top with a strategically placed hole through which one breast, fortunately clad in black lace, protrudes. I ponder their motivation, give up, and turn my thoughts to the predictably bewildered reaction of the Greek parents, who are probably struggling very hard to give their sons a foreign education. The sacred tradition of Greek hospitality is about to be strained to breaking-point. All these parents will be able to do is be polite, kind, generous; say their prayers; pour libations, and hope that these romances are mere passing whims, boys sowing their wild oats.

Adjustments are always difficult, even though I am reunited with my children and with milder weather. The household is, of course, irredeemably macho (even poor old Ozzie is male), and at the beginning, during the difficult time of re-entry into the atmosphere,

I struggle to assert myself; after a very short interval such efforts seem to be a waste of time, so that I return to my endeavour to think worthy and improving thoughts while washing the inevitable khaki socks. People who lead one life in one place and one culture often find it difficult to understand the points of view of people who shift uneasily between two or more, and give no credit for knowledge and experience gained in any world but their own.

When the news comes that Mick is to spend six months with the peace-keeping forces in Bosnia, I am quite alone in my reaction. I sit and cry quietly while everybody else is running around gleefully. I get short shrift from Tom. 'Don't start, for God's sake! Why can't you be happy for him?' One's children are often the most unfamiliar of strangers, after all. 'I congratulate him, because he wants to go, but don't ask me to be happy,' is all the reply I can manage.

The olive harvest is upon us again. Mick has left; Jo has important exams to prepare for. The hapless Tom I have to pull from bed every morning, almost by the big toe, while he moans his protests. I slip into the Pollyanna mode which so irritates him.

'Be glad we've got some machinery now. Be glad the Albanians are here to help. Be glad the sun is shining.'

'Yeah.'

But still he complains, so I have to wheel out the big guns and remind him of his ancestors and their land and trees and his inheritance and his father and brothers and the consequent responsibility. (What a prig. What a pain in the neck I am, but I've got to get him out of bed and into the olive groves somehow.)

'Yeah, all *right*. That's enough. I've got the message.'

And he sighs the sigh of one who knows that fate cannot be avoided or escaped, and so we start our hard work. It used to be harder, as I have said, but now the pure and silent air of this beautiful countryside is threatened by solid-fuel-powered chainsaws and olive-strippers. 'Everything changes,' an Athenian remarked to me recently. 'You can't stop progress.' But I don't like change, and is this progress? I wonder, while spending six hours a day beating olives off branches, wrecking ageing hands, wrists and shoulders in the process. Once more I think of the House of Lords and chuckle ruefully.

Tom has the most tedious job, that of using a machine to strip the olive branches. He stands for hours, bending and lifting and placing boughs against revolving cylinders while the machine whines and stray olives soar into the air, at which point we all duck, a full-speed olive being a dangerous and painful missile. He becomes, understandably, very tired, and starts to moan once more. 'If I win the lottery, I'll never do this again.'

'Whatever happened to the spirit of Anzac?' I ask, hoping to raise a laugh.

He grins. 'Don't look at me.'

It is nearly Christmas. This feast, not nearly as important as Easter in the Greek Orthodox calendar, is beginning to take on some of the commercial significance it has had for years in Western culture. Thirty years ago it was practically impossible to find a Christmas tree; now they are everywhere. Canned Christmas carols are played in the shops, and decorations have proliferated to an alarming degree.

But the Christmas Eve custom persists; early in

the morning children come in groups to sing '*Ta Kalanda*', which announces the arrival of Christ. A different version heralds the arrival of St Basil, and is sung on New Year's Eve. The march of time being what it is, Tom, Mick and Jo no longer rise at the crack of dawn to greet the singers in high excitement, as they did when they were much younger; now bedroom doors are firmly shut against the ritual enquiry, *Na ta poume?* (Will we sing it?)

Christmas weather varies, and I for one do not need much in the way of frost or rain to decide not to go to the liturgy, which starts at six o'clock in the morning. The first Christmas that Tom was away studying in Australia I was utterly miserable, missing him badly, and the weather certainly did not lend itself to any spontaneous outbursts of Christmas cheer. Gale-force winds ripped and tore at everything: doors and shutters had to be wedged shut lest they be wrenched open, and we thumbtacked huge pieces of reinforced silver foil over the bottom half of the French windows in order to stop some of the draughts, which were not draughts so much as hurricanes. The high winds meant that the wood stove could not be lit. The noise was simply tremendous, and every so often the wind sounded like a lunatic voice, howling and shrieking, cutting us and the house off from outside contact. Of course the phone went dead. The darkness and gloom were such that I really felt as if I were learning what it would be like to be battened down in a sailing ship.

A Greek friend told me later that she had felt as if she were in her coffin; she became so claustrophobic and breathless during the night that she promptly decided she would be cremated, an extremely radical decision for a member of the Greek Orthodox Church to make. Her ashes are to be scattered in the sea: no coffin, no box in the charnel-house for her. It seems ironic that the Nativity had made us think of death and disaster.

Another Christmastide Jo and I were in England, in the north. Jo had never had an Australian Christmas, and the English one meant a whole range of new experiences. He had never seen frost on fields at three o'clock in the afternoon, had never heard his boots crunch and crackle on a rimed path. He looked carefully, I remember, at the minute, separate splinters of ice sitting on the tops of the fences, at each holly leaf edged in white, at frozen cobwebs like so many starched doyleys hung out to dry on hedges and walls.

Neither Jo nor I had ever seen a frozen pond before. He stood quite still to look at the sheet of blue glass set in an intricate, faceted framework of trees and bushes powdered with white. He bent and stared at the greenery, the trails of weed trapped beneath the ice, and could not believe the sight of a frozen frog just under the surface. Later the Tyne was frozen, too, except for a channel in mid-stream. Thin sheets of ice sat like broken panes at the edge of the river, and a pair of herons flew in a slow, dignified fashion before they disappeared into the feathery foliage of the trees. We both learned about the colours of white, steel, slate, pale pink and pearl, which are so different from the boldness of Greek blues and ultramarines, and the mixture of garishness and tints which are the colours of Australia.

I took Jo to the pantomime *Dick Whittington and his Cat*. He was much younger then, but his Greek machismo was definitely budding, if not in bloom. It hadn't occurred to me to instruct him in the niceties of the English pantomime tradition, with the result that no sooner had the curtain risen than a shaking finger pointed at the stage and its owner gasped, 'He's, it's, Dick's a woman!' Further frights followed. 'Sarah the Cook's a man!' For a little while after that, whenever the lights went up for some audience participation, he could be seen anxiously perusing the programme for further evidence of cross-dressing.

Christmas Day comes and goes and can never be as it was, now that the boys are turning into men, men with a gypsy mother.

It is suddenly the last day of the year and I take Ozzie for a walk behind the village. He creaks along, a shadow of his former self, and that makes two of us. The weather is very mild, and although the death knell has tolled for three people in the week I've been back, today it is impossible to think of an end to anything. The olive harvest is still in progress and this in itself is the peasant world's guarantee of life. Voices call back and forth, chainsaws buzz, and the tapping of sticks produces the spatter of falling olives. Donkeys fret and stamp. Purple irises are growing wild, the chrysanthemums are blooming in a late blaze of yellow, and here and there a bougainvillea is still in flower. Smoke drifts across the valley. There is a conspiracy of beauty in Greece, and I become ensnared in the plot every time I am here; I just wish that I did not always leave with the feeling of having been rubbed all over with sandpaper.

I return from my walk to news of yet another death in the village. The deceased is a man who has not reached old age, who spent part of his life in Sydney and whose daughter married an Aborigine.

In the afternoon I plant broccoli seeds and do not know why: I will not be here to eat any of the broccoli that struggles to growth.

Jo accompanies me to a New Year's Eve party at a mansion in a nearby town and is bored to sobs while I, usual depressive spiral somehow suspended, count fur coats, try to pretend I'm not staring at the jewellery, and observe the dyed hair on women of about my own age. A deep burgundy seems to be the favoured shade this winter.

A desperately unhappy woman is present; I deduce

she is saddled with an impossible but rich husband. At suppertime they sit at separate tables, and he never once acknowledges her presence. She makes valiant efforts at conversation for a brief space and then lapses into the silence of misery and simply sits, not even picking at the food in front of her. Sitting next to her is her only son, and her sad face lights up every time she looks at him. The concentration of affection, even passion, on a child seems to be part of the pattern of relationships in rural Greece, and is often the result of arranged marriages which have been disappointments.

In the middle of finery and affluence the house-keeper flutters about, waiting on the guests. Her hair is tumbling down her back in a great mane, and she wears a red apron and turquoise bedroom slippers, fluffy ones. 'I'd rather be with the babies,' whispers Jo. 'New Year's Eve is always grim,' I say selfishly. 'Count the fur coats and be glad I'm getting all this copy.' He helps himself to another Coca-Cola.

Sun is streaming into my room as I open my eyes on New Year's Day, the Feast of St Basil, and my first thought is, The start of another year without my mother. And without my sister. I lie blinking while the scorpions of loss slither in my mind.

Tom is here; he, too, thinks that New Year's Eve is the worst night of the year. At least my children seem to be free of the pernicious effects of romanticism and idealism, despite having an ageing Romantic Idealist for a mother. 'Any resolutions?' I ask Tom and Jo. 'Nah,' they reply in unison. Sensible, I consider.

Mine are of the negative variety: I resolve to have no resolutions, I plan to have no plans. I wonder instead where exactly Mick is and what he is doing. *Tempus fugit* awfully fast, I tell myself: it won't be too long before he's back again. But in the meantime there is the fact of absence and its influence. It is very hard to estimate the degree of effect absence has, and one's ego is nearly always involved, but I know the thought that I should be with him for the new year haunts me. Wanderers regularly feel they should be where they are not.

I consider the subject of my sons. Well, I'm always doing this. I consider what they are, and have decided that they are Australian Greeks; were they living in

Australia they would be Greek Australians. Their lives have not been easy, and no doubt will not be in the future. But because they have a dual heritage they are able to cheat the boredom and the limitations that are often the lot of people born into only one culture. Their psyches, it seems to me, have an inbuilt pendulum and so they can be Greeks in Greece and Australians in Australia, can see both cultures as subjects rather than objects – a happy state of affairs quite beyond my grasp. Belonging to both, they have the capacity to be clear-eyed about both, an ability which I know now will always elude me. For them, the comparisons and contrasts are internalised. Myself, I have to be content with bilingual dreams.

I sit here on the balcony. The sun is shining so brightly that I have had to shed my jacket. A cobweb is glinting in the light. Today I have been lucky: for the very first time, the coin in the *vasilopita,* the New Year cake, is mine. It is a five-drachma piece dated 1980, the year I came to Greece, supposedly for six months' holiday. I wish myself a happy new year.

At night I am on the balcony again. Perhaps it is not surprising that I think once more of that sufferer

Richard Mahony, who had the sensibilities of both set-
tler and nomad jostling within the one psyche. Quite
early in the novel he says, 'Never forget that, whatever
happens, there *is* a sky, with stars in it, above us.'

I look up to the thick clusters in the sky over the
Peloponnese and tell myself that it should not matter
greatly whether I can see the Southern Cross or not.
It is probably too early in the year, but I gaze at the
studded blackness and tell myself that I can see Leo
and the Heavenly Twins instead.